KETO INSTANT POT COOKBOOK

The Complete Ketogenic Diet Instant Pot
Cookbook – Healthy, Quick & Easy Keto
Instant Pot Recipes for Everyone

By
WILLIAM COOK

Disclaimer and Terms of Use:

Effort has been made to ensure that the information in this book is accurate and complete, however, the author and the publisher do not warrant the accuracy of the information, text and graphics contained within the book due to the rapidly changing nature of science, research, known and unknown facts and internet. The Author and the publisher do not hold any responsibility for errors, omissions or contrary interpretation of the subject matter herein. This book is presented solely for motivational and informational purposes only.

TABLE OF CONTENTS

INTRODUCTION

The ketogenic diet, which is gaining immense popularity all around the world, is a high-fat diet. Unlike other diet plans, which focus on low-fat consumption, the ketogenic diet is something different. It is a new approach to maintain a perfect body with some little flaws. The ketogenic diet involves reducing or entirely cutting the intake of carbohydrates, which leads to a metabolic condition in the body generally termed as Ketosis.

With some astounding benefits, the ketogenic diet is not harmful to our body. It has less risk and disease factors as compared to other diets. People are now showing a keen interest in keto diet as it burns fat 2.2 times more than a regular diet, which restricts calories and fat. Not only keto diet helps in losing weight, but it also helps in improving the Triglyceride and HDL Cholesterol levels. Apart from astonishing weight loss benefits, the ketogenic diet has tremendously adapted by the cancer patients to treat tumors.

It is quite surprising and wonderful to note that keto diet severely reduces the symptoms of Alzheimer's disease and slows down its development. Not only this, how can one even imagine that keto diet can also help in reducing acne? Acne and breakouts are definitely an issue but all thanks to the ketogenic diet for reducing acne drastically. The risk of heart disease also appears decidedly less once people start using a ketogenic diet. The low-carb or no-carb diet is bliss and ecstasy for everyone.

If you are on a mission of "losing weight" and "being healthy" all the time, then this book is what you need in your life. Get the delicious and variety of ketogenic diet recipes that are not only luscious but are nutritious and salubrious too!

CHAPTER 1: THE KETOGENIC DIET

What Is the Ketogenic diet?

A food procedure by which you may lose weight by lowering your requirement of carbohydrates is the critical principle in the ketogenic diet. By consuming lower carbs, a moderate amount of protein and vitamins, the body produces energy from the stored fat. In this way, the body generates energy from the keto body or fat that burns to produce calories.

Human beings produce ketones when the liver stimulates the fat to produce energy. Generally, when you are in a ketogenic diet, then the body switches to a state when the body runs on fuel, mostly by burning fats. It helps to reduce the fat content of the body leading to a leaner and healthier individual. The brain stimulates a sensation of hunger, and it is produced either from carbohydrates or from fats. While losing weight, starving is the best possible way, but literary that's impossible. Remember, if you live on a keto diet for a longer time, it will result in ketosis.

While you are on a ketogenic diet, you will consume all types of available fats, non-starchy vegetables, fruits, dairy products and a decidedly lesser amount of carbohydrates. You have to follow a meticulous routine where you may consume seafood, chicken and other meat, but avoid food made from white flour, semolina, wheat, and rice. In fact, the ideal weight comes from 60-75% fat, 15-30% protein, and 5-10% carbohydrates. You may emphasize keto drinks and keto alcohol and opt for a small trial, say, for 7 days or 14 days to see if the keto diet is working on you or not.

What You Can Eat

The ketogenic diet is a food plan based on low amount of carbohydrates, high fats, a moderate amount of proteins and other essential minerals. The whole idea is about breaking the stored fat of the body for energy instead of carbohydrates. When the body depends on fat for energy, the fat deposit mobilizes and leads to weight loss. During ketosis, your body starts burning fat for energy resulting in weight loss.

It is possible for the body to switch to ketosis mode that is determined by a simple urine test. Once ketosis is attained, the body starts burning fats instead of glucose.

When the amount of carbohydrates becomes low in the body, the liver converts the fats to fatty acids and ketone bodies. The keto bodies pass to the brain thereby replacing glucose as the energy source. Ideally, a keto diet has 60-75% fat, 15-30% protein, and 5-10% carbohydrates.

There are certain things that you can eat and a lot that are in the 'Not to eat' list. Let's check out all the things that you can eat in this read.

> **Meat:** You can relish all non-processed meats. Naturally obtained meat is highly recommendable. Since keto is a high-fat, moderate amount of protein and a negligible amount of carbs diet plan, you can have an inconsiderable amount of meat. As per the keto

diet plan, 60-75 percent of calorie requirement will meet from fat, which you can get from meat and other sources too. Beef, chicken, pork, and lamb are highly preferred, and you may check various recipes with permutation combination of these, and bring justice to your taste buds.

Seafood and fish: All types of sea fishes are appropriate except those that are cultured. All you may depend on is the wild caught sea fishes. Cultured fishes contain a lot of carbohydrates, so they are not preferable. Go for salmon, tuna, herrings and any other kind of seafood.

Eggs: Eggs are the most recommended food in this type of diet, and they can be consumed in any form, be it scrambled, hard-boiled or parboiled. Make sure that you choose organic or pastured eggs instead of that bread by poultry. The consumption of eggs is restricted to 3-6 per day, but you can consume lesser than this amount.

Natural fats, high-fat sources: It's a corollary that the energy obtained on a keto diet should come from fats. Although you can get it in natural sources like fish, meat, and eggs, still you may prefer to take fats from other sources like coconut oil, butter, olive oil, etc. You may add a dollop of butter or olive oil over salads.

Vegetables that grow above the ground: You can meticulously eat all vegetables that grow above the ground. Since vegetables, which grow below the ground, contain a high amount of carbohydrates, you should avoid those items. Eat a lot of broccoli, cauliflower, turnips, cabbage, spinach, coriander, zucchini, avocado, eggplants, carrot, and onions.

High-fat dairy products: All those fats that you can get from dairies like butter, cheese, ghee, high-fat heavy crème can be consumed and used in cooking. You may choose to use them almost every day.

Nuts: You may eat nuts but in moderate levels. Although you can consume nuts as a snack, it's better to eat them while hungry instead of having any carb rich or junk foods. Choose out of pecans, walnuts, peanuts, almonds, sunflower seeds and macadamia that will give you energy and enhance your brain health.

Berries: You may opt for berries during your diet but in small amounts of them. Types of berries that you can try are strawberries, cranberries, and blueberries. You may try them with whipping crème which is a very popular dessert in keto diet.

Drinks: If you're following a keto diet, then you must drink lots of water. Having water with slices of lemon or lime is good as it works as a detoxing agent. In case you are suffering from a headache or keto flu, then try adding a few pinches of salt to your drink. You may consume coffee and tea without sugar. Bone broth can be added to your list of drinks while you are on a keto diet.

What You Can't Eat

The ketogenic diet is a food practice that consists of a minimum amount of carbs and high fat intake. The mechanism is very simple, when you consume a low amount of carbs, your body adapts to a state of ketosis. For energy, your body starts burning fat.

To what extent you can limit the intake of carbs? For an exact answer to the question, you shall consult with a dietitian or a doctor, who can guide you to set a minimum limit of your carb intake. Actually, the minimum level of carbs intake varies from person to person. If you want to put your body in a state of ketosis vigorously, then limit the net carb intake less than 10g per serve. For most people, going under 35 grams of total carbs per day is enough to reach ketosis.

The ketogenic diet is hard to do and adapt in our everyday life. However, making it a habit takes only 21 days. The ketogenic diet is not just about food and no-carb thing. There are so many things, which get a 'BIG No' from the keto diet. Not only the intake of fat increases but also the banned food list of the keto diet is also enormous. Here is the list of items, which one should not only avoid but also restrict if they are on a ketogenic diet:

- **Fruits** – Keto diet strictly restricts the intake of fruits like apples, bananas, oranges, grapes, and watermelons. Not only this, there are many other fruits, like pineapple, cherries, peach, melon, pears, lemon, grapefruit, plums, mango, etc., are limited on a ketogenic diet.

- **Grain Products** – Products like cereal, bread, pasta, rice, corn, oatmeal, etc., have no place in the ketogenic diet. Along with these, crackers, pizza, popcorn, granola, bagels, muesli, and flour are also not allowed on the keto diet.

- **A big NO to chocolates** – Sweets like candy, chocolate, cakes, buns, and pastries are not allowed on the keto diet. Other sweets such as tarts, pies, ice cream, cookies, pudding, and custard also should be kept out of your plate.

- **Dips and sweet sauces** – Sweet sauces like ketchup, BBQ sauce, and tomato sauce are restricted. Some salad dressings and hot sauces are also not allowed on this diet plan.

- **No to Alcohol** – Beverages that include alcohol like beer, cider, sweet wines, and sweetened alcoholic drinks should not be consumed during a ketogenic diet.

- **Dairy products** – Dairy products like skim milk, mozzarella cheese, fat-free yogurt, low cheese, and cream cheese are not allowed on a ketogenic diet.

- **Grains** – Grains like wheat, rice, rye, and oats are not preferable on a keto diet. Other products including corn, quinoa, barley, millet, bulgur, amaranth, buckwheat, and sprouted grains are not allowed too.

- **Sweet Drinks** - No smoothies, juice, sweetened tea, soda, and coffee are allowed when you are on a ketogenic diet.

- **A big NO to sweets** - Maple syrup, sugar cane agave nectar, Splenda, aspartame, honey saccharin, and corn syrup, etc., should not be consumed when one is undergoing a keto diet plan.

Benefits of the Ketogenic Diet

Indeed, the ketogenic diet is a bolt out of blue of all the weight loss diets we discuss in social media and all health magazines these days. It's all about removing unnecessary carbohydrate-based food but instead packs it with protein, essential vitamins, and, of course, fats. The main idea is switching to a ketosis mode where the energy is derived primarily from fats and not carbohydrates. Many people observed quick and effective results following a ketogenic diet.

- Ketogenic diet leads to reduced inflammation by the production of free radicals whereby the body uses ketones to produce energy instead of glucose.

- The slow process of ketogenic diet leads to burning of fat. Researchers say that the procedure of high-fat low carb diet is far effective than low-fat, high carb diet. In fact, a ketogenic diet leads to improved lipid profiles thereby promoting weight loss.

- While you are on a ketogenic diet, your mental clarity improves. Neurological inflammation leads to depression, but a ketogenic diet helps to improve the neurological conditions leading to improved mental health.

- You will observe that when you are following a ketogenic diet, you will have abundant energy. The simple reason being is lowered inflammation, regulation of mitochondrial biogenesis and production of more ATP molecules from ketones compared to glucose.

- Following a ketogenic diet will lead to clearer skin. In case you are suffering from eczema, psoriasis or acne, your condition will definitely improve once you go for a keto diet. It also helps you lower inflammation and hence it will accelerate healing.

- When you opt for a ketogenic diet, you can reduce your hunger pangs and cravings for meals. A ketosis state of mind provides the brain with stable energy and eliminates unhealthy food cravings.

- A keto diet leads to mitochondrial biogenesis. As most of us are using glucose for energy generation, switching to the fat burning mode is evident after the body is in ketosis mode. At this point, the cell develops new mitochondria and elevates energy production.

- The mitochondrial genesis leads to energy production and elevated level of gene expression. Scientists say that following a ketogenic diet can actually lead to anti-aging. By prolonged fasting, it will promote mitochondrial health and also biogenesis.

- Researchers say that a keto diet leads to reduced tendencies of chronic diseases like cancer, depression, anxiety, autism, chronic fatigue, diabetes, and heart-related disease.

- It has revealed in a study that keto diet boosts mental health. People who have bipolar disorders, anxiety, schizophrenia, and depression often benefit from following a ketogenic diet.

- If you follow keto diet, then your sexual health will improve leading to an increased urge in sex drive. Dietary fat intake and sex hormones do have inherent connections. High-fat diet often increases the estrogen level in women leading to a higher sex drive. For women who are nearing menopause, keto diet is a must as estrogen levels are plummeting this point of time.

In a nutshell, we can conclude that living on a ketogenic diet not only promotes weight loss but also reduces the risk of many common diseases. You will experience lower cholesterol, low blood pressure, and low blood sugar and also reduced appetite, including triglycerides.

CHAPTER 2: INSTANT POT

What Is an Instant Pot?

An instant pot is a smart electric cooking appliance, also known as a versatile multi-cooker that can be used for pressure cooking, rice cooking, slow cooking, high pressure cooking, steaming, simmering, sautéing, searing, warming, yogurt making, pre-programmed and customized cooking, and much more. Such instant pots shall not only save up space in your kitchen but also the cooking time as well.

Instant pots come with specially designed multiple preset cooking options that can meet various types of cooking, like slow cooking, high-pressure cooking and various other types of cuisine, from meat cooking to cake making.

The magic became real after different preset programs were made to cook the food at a higher perfection level. Although instant pots invented years back, today the demand for the cooking appliance is very high, because of the convenient multiple options and safety features.

Operating the instant pot is very simple. Each cooking appliance comes with the user's manual, which will let you understand the different working mechanism and also some manufacturers offer free instant pot recipes as a complimentary gift making cooking a hassle-free experience.

Reading further the book lets you have some general idea about cooking on instant pot and also exploring through the various instant pot recipes will let you enjoy the ease of cooking. Before you crash land on to the recipe section, read further to have basic knowledge about instant pot.

How to Use Your Instant Pot?

Before understanding about how to use an instant pot, you should know about the pot setup process, which is the basic one must learn before handling an instant pot.

Washing the accessories:

Keep ready all the essential accessories of instant pot before starting the cooking process. We shall deal with the rest of the accessories on due course. Make sure to give a warm soapy water wash to accessories like inner pot, silicon sealing ring, and lid and to the other items before preparing your favourite recipes.

Twisting the lids:

The very first skill you must master before using an instant pot is about the opening and closing of lid with ease. Twist the lid counter-clockwise until the inverted triangle gets aligned with the other unlocked triangle sign to open the cover. To close the lid, reverse the motion as mentioned above. With continuous practice, anyone can quickly get used to this particular mechanism.

Keeping the sealing ring properly:

In most of the instant pots, the sealing rings are silicone made. You have to ensure that the sealing rings appropriately seated within the lid. The sealing ring must sit tight within the lid, so that the food gets properly cooked. Also, make sure to clean the sealing ring from time to time to clear previously prepared food odors.

Checking with other parts on the lid:

Make sure the venting knob, which is also known as the instant pot steam release valve is fully attached within the lid and pushed downwards before start cooking.

The instant pot float valve which can be found near to the venting knob must easily pop up and down to go easy with the pressure levels.

The anti-block shield must be pushed to the sides to lift it and can be pushed down to install it back.

Installing condensation collector:

The condensation collector is a must to install before plugging in the instant pot to a power source. The slot to connect the collector can be found on the back part of the instant pot. Just slide in the collector, and it gets easily fixed to the instant pot.

With the basic instant pot setup process covered, let's move on to the instant pot buttons that can be used to control the way you want to cook the food.

The six basic instant pot buttons:

Although there are more than sixteen buttons present depending on the model of the instant pots, below mentioned are the six necessary buttons that can go easy with your cooking process.

1. **Manual button:**

   The manual switch can be used to set up your required pressure cooking time. You can set a maximum of two hundred and forty minutes by using the manual button.

2. **"+" and "-" button:**

   You can use these two buttons to increase or decrease your overall cooking time or the timer.

3. **Adjust button:**

   By pressing this button, you can change from the default cooking settings to an advanced level. If this button is not present in the model you have purchased, then you can double press the 'sauté' button to enable the same mechanism.

4. **Sauté button:**

   As the same denotes, you can use the 'sauté' button to brown, sauté or even simmer the ingredients present inside the pot with or without closing the lid.

5. **Cancel or Keep Warm button:**

   Press this button to either turn off the pot or to move towards a keep warm function, during which the food stays in a warm condition, without further cooking until you serve.

6. **Timer button:**

It is an ideal setting to set up the required time to cook the food. A maximum of twenty-four hours can be set in the timer. The food will get cooked as per the set temperature and cease the cooking upon elapsing the time.

Pressure release valve and its functionality:

Instant pot comes with two types of pressure release system, and they are Natural Pressure Release (NPR) and Quick Pressure Release (QRR). While using an instant pot, your food shall never get prepared entirely by setting up a timer. You also need to learn the two different pressure release functions, which are required to use when you needed to get some unique cooking effect.

1. **Performing a quick pressure release:**

Once the pre-setup cooking time elapses, you need to move the venting knob away from the sealing position to release the pressure quickly. The quick release valve is easy to operate. You need to just release the valve as per the instant pot instruction, where a recipe requires to perform quick pressure release. After releasing the valve, you need to wait until the metal pin (floating valve) drops down completely, before opening the lid.

The advantage of using a quick pressure release:

QPR is a great option to completely stop the entire cooking process and to prevent the food from getting overcooked. This pressure release goes easy while cooking vegetables like bok choy, broccoli, and corn and even with seafood like crab, salmon, and lobster.

2. **Performing a natural pressure release:**

In this process, after your desired cooking cycle gets finished, you need to wait until the metal pin (floating value) drops down entirely before opening up the lid. Always make sure to turn the venting knob from the sealing towards the venting position to make sure the pressure gets evenly released before opening up the cover. The natural pressure release may take about ten to twenty minutes to get the force wholly relieved, and release will depend on the amount of food getting cooked under pressure.

The advantage of using a natural pressure release:

If you are preparing a foamy food or the ones that require substantial levels of liquid volumes (e.g., congee, porridge, soup, etc.), then natural pressure release is a great option. As the pressure is gradually released, less movement happens within the pressure cooker, leading to no spills from occurring around the pot.

What Are the Benefits of Using the Instant Pot?

It has multiple benefits, and the main advantages are saving overall cooking time, and conserving energy. Below are some of the detailed information on the benefits and advantages of using instant pot on a daily basis.

Saving precious time:

Instant pot shall not only prepare your recipes efficiently but also does save valuable time. When you use the pre-set options, it works like a 'fill it-forget it' mode. It won't let overcooking, and the integrated circuit system and sensors manage the entire cooking process and stop further cooking after the pre-set time elapses. After cooking, it shifts to warm mode, automatically.

Some instant pots come with 4-hour automatic warm option, allows you to enjoy warm food. Similarly, if you opt for slow cooking, it is useful to manage the cooking time effectively. You can set your cooking before bed or before going to the office. Your food will be ready by the time you want to have it, and it will be warm too. Thanks to the automatic warm options. No need to worry about overcooking.

The inner pots of instant pot come insulated which allow to instantly start the cooking process, ending up saving your time and energy. The insulation allows quick heat conductivity, and hence the cooking begins immediately.

Instant pot requires less liquid levels to cook the food when compared to traditional cooking appliances. The low liquid level helps to prepare the food faster and keep the food in the required consistency state.

When compared with other types of cooking methods, the instant pot cooking can save your cooking time and energy bills up to seventy percentage.

Retains nutrients and vitamins from the ingredients:

The food will lose its nutritional values under direct boiling process. By pressure cooking using an instant pot, you can not only cook your food at a faster time rate but also let all the ingredients stay within the food. Since the food gets prepared with a closed chamber, it ensures the vitamins and other nutrients present in the ingredients to evenly spread and remain with the food, as there is the limited scope of steam evaporation.

Preserves the taste:

Cooking in an open container shall expose the added ingredients to higher oxidation which will considerably reduce original flavor. Also cooking in the open container shall evaporate the nutritional values too. Preparing foods in an instant pot will keep the flavor of the ingredients intact as there is no oxidation happens and hence the original character will get preserved with the meal. Similarly, as there are no open cooking, and minimum possibilities of evaporation, all the nutritional values will stay with the cooked food.

Other than just following up with the basic steps to prepare your meal, you can be creative and do a variety of cooking experiments by using an instant pot. The pre-programmed cooking option can cut your cooking time and save energy bills.

CHAPTER 3:
MEASUREMENT CONVERSIONS

US Dry Volume Measurements

1/16 teaspoon	Dash
1/8 teaspoon	Pinch
3 teaspoons	1 tablespoon
1/8 cup	2 tablespoons (1 standard coffee scoop)
1/4 cup	4 tablespoons
1/3 cup	5 tablespoons plus 1 teaspoon
1/2 cup	8 tablespoons
3/4 cup	12 tablespoons
1 cup	16 tablespoons
1 pound	16 ounces

US liquid volume measurements

8 Fluid ounces	1 Cup
1 Pint	2 Cups (16 fluid ounces)
1 Quart	2 Pints (4 cups)
1 Gallon	4 Quarts (16 cups)

US to Metric Conversions

1/5 teaspoon	1 ml (ml stands for milliliter, one thousandth of a liter)
1 teaspoon	5 ml
1 tablespoon	15 ml
1 fluid oz.	30 ml
1/5 cup	50 ml
1 cup	240 ml
2 cups (1 pint)	470 ml
4 cups (1 quart)	.95 liter
4 quarts (1 gal)	3.8 liters
1 oz.	28 grams
1 pound	454 grams

Metric to US Conversions

1 milliliter	1/5 teaspoon
5 ml	1 teaspoon
15 ml	1 tablespoon
30 ml	1 fluid oz.
100 ml	3.4 fluid oz.
240 ml	1 cup
1 liter	34 fluid oz.
1 liter	4.2 cups
1 liter	2.1 pints
1 liter	1.06 quarts
1 liter	.26 gallon
1 gram	.035 ounce
100 grams	3.5 ounces
500 grams	1.10 pounds
1 kilogram	2.205 pounds
1 kilogram	35 oz.

Temperature Conversions

Fahrenheit	Celsius	Gas Mark
275° F	140° C	gas mark 1 - cool
300° F	150° C	gas mark 2
325° F	165° C	gas mark 3 - very moderate
350° F	180° C	gas mark 4 - moderate
375° F	190° C	gas mark 5
400° F	200° C	gas mark 6 - moderately hot
425° F	220° C	gas mark 7 - hot
450° F	230° C	gas mark 9
475° F	240° C	gas mark 10 - very hot

Abbreviations

Cooking Abbreviation(s)	Unit of Measurement
C, c	cup
g	gram
kg	kilogram
L, l	liter
lb	pound
mL, ml	milliliter
oz	ounce
pt	pint
t, tsp	teaspoon
T, TB, Tbl, Tbsp	tablespoon

CHAPTER 4: KETOGENIC RECIPES

EGGS AND VEGETABLES

INSTANT POT CREAMY SCRAMBLED EGGS

Preparation: 5 minutes | Cooking: 15 minutes | Serves: 1

Ingredients:

- Grass-Fed Butter - 1 tablespoon
- Large Eggs - 2
- Heavy Cream - 1 tablespoon
- Salt – as per taste
- Ground Black Pepper - as per need
- Sharp Cheddar Cheese shredded – ½ ounce
- Chives (optional) - for garnish

Cooking directions:

1. Set your Instant Pot to Sauté mode and press to start.

2. Add butter and heat it until it melts and starts to make bubbles.

3. While it is melting, in a large bowl beat together the cream, eggs, salt, and pepper until it becomes smooth and creamy.

4. Now pour the mixture into heated Instant Pot.

5. Scatter the whole cheese on top and let it seated in the pan, for about 25 - 30 seconds.

6. With the use of a silicone spatula, fold up the edges of the eggs towards the middle of the pot. Carry on your scrambling in this manner (scraping melted cheese into the eggs), until the eggs boiled with firmness. The cheese will get pretty tight in the meantime.

7. Once the cheese becomes tight, press stop.

8. Now serve hot with sprinkling freshly chop upped chives.

Nutritional values: Calories: 353 | Total Fats: 31g | Net Carbs: 1g | Protein: 18g | Fiber: 1g | Cholesterol: 437mg | Sodium: 337mg | Potassium: 163mg

INSTANT POT BREAKFAST EGG CASSEROLE

Preparation time: 10 minutes | Cooking: 35 minutes | Serves: 6

Ingredients:

- Eggs – 6 large
- Garlic, minced – 6 cloves
- Broccoli stalks, chafed – 3 medium
- Avocado oil – 2 tablespoon
- Heavy cream - ¼ cups
- Cheese (Monterey Jack), shredded – 1 cup
- Avocado, sliced – 1
- Onion green, finely chopped – 1
- Breakfast bulk sausage – 6 ounces
- Salsa, sour cream, extra cheese for serving.
- Salt and pepper to taste

Cooking method:

1. Take a 7-inch casserole and grease it.
2. Put on your Instant Pot to Sauté mode.
3. Pour avocado oil.
4. When oil becomes hot, add bulk sausage and break it by using a wooden spatula.
5. Cook it until its pink color disappears. It may take about 4 minutes.
6. Now add the chafed broccoli, garlic, salt and pepper as per your taste.
7. Continue cooking for about 2 minutes until the broccoli becomes soft.
8. Transfer the entire mix to the casserole.
9. Now take a medium bowl and combine cream and eggs.
10. Add onion and cheese and continue stirring.
11. Transfer the mix over the sausage mix in the casserole.
12. Cover the casserole with an aluminum foil.
13. Now pour 1 cup of water into the bottom of the Instant Pot and place the trivet.
14. Keep the casserole over the trivet and close the lid.
15. Close the vent and set the Instant Pot to manual pressure cook for 25 minutes.
16. After 25 minutes, let the cooker release the pressure naturally for 10 minutes.
17. After 10 minutes release the remaining pressure manually.
18. Open the lid and remove the dish.
19. Top the dish with finely sliced avocado.
20. Top it with salsa, sour cream, and extra cheese as you wish.
21. Serve hot.

Nutritional values: Calories: 351 | Carbs: 6.8g | Fiber: 2.9g | Protein: 19.6g

INSTANT POT KETO POBLANO CHEESE FRITTATA

Preparation: 10 minutes | Cooking: 30 minutes | Serves: 4

Ingredients:

- Eggs - 4
- Diced canned green chilies – 10 ounces
- Mexican blend shredded cheese divided – 1 cup
- Ground cumin - ½ teaspoon
- Chopped cilantro - ¼ cup
- Half and Half (any equivalent) - 1 cup
- Salt - ½ or 1 teaspoon
- Water – 2 cups

Cooking directions:

1. In a bowl beat eggs thoroughly.
2. Blend the beaten eggs with diced green chilies and Half and Half.
3. Add cumin and salt into the mixture.
4. Pour half cup of shredded cheese into the mixture and mix it well.
5. Now, set the Instant Pot to Sauté mode.
6. Press start for cooking in low medium heat.
7. When the pot become hot, pour the mixture into it.
8. Cover the pot with aluminum foil.
9. Now, pour two cups of water in the instant pot.
10. Place a trivet on it and place the pot over it.
11. Close the lid and set the Instant Pot to manual high pressure cook for twenty minutes.
12. Let the pressure release naturally for the next ten minutes and release the remaining pressure manually.
13. Now, take the leftover cheese and spread it over the tart.
14. After that place it under a hot broiler for about five minutes.
15. Heat it until the cheese becomes brown.
16. Serve hot.

Nutritional values: Calories: 257 | Total Fat: 19g | Saturated Fat: 10g | Total Carbohydrates: 6g | Protein: 14g | Dietary Fiber: 1g

KETO CHEESE-CRUSTED OMELET

Preparation: 5 minutes | Cooking: 5 minutes | Serves: 1

Ingredients:

For omelet:

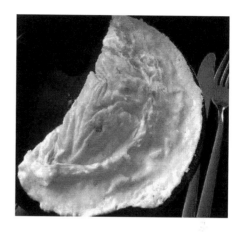

- Eggs – 2
- Heavy whipping cream – 2 tablespoons
- Butter or coconut oil – 1 tablespoon
- Salt
- Ground black pepper
- Mature shredded cheese or sliced – 2½ ounces

For Filling:

- Mushrooms, sliced – 2
- Cherry tomatoes, sliced – 2
- Cream cheese – 2 tablespoons
- Baby spinach – ½ ounce
- Deli turkey – 1 ounce
- Dried oregano – 1 teaspoon

Cooking directions:

1. Add eggs, salt, pepper, and cream in a bowl and mix well.
2. Set the Instant Pot to sauté mode.
3. Add a dollop of butter in the insert pot and heat it on medium low temperature.
4. Let the cheese spread evenly in the bottom. Continue heating until it becomes bubbly.
5. Now, put the entire egg mixture over it and heat it on low temperature. Do not stir and let it cook for a few minutes.
6. Add mushrooms, tomatoes, turkey, oregano, cream cheese and baby spinach on half portion of the omelet.
7. Cook the egg mixture for a few more minutes and wait until it starts to harden.
8. Now, put the empty half over the other filled half and flip it.
9. Cook for a few more minutes and serve hot.

Nutritional values: Calories: 789 | Fat: 66g | Net Carbohydrates: 8g | Fiber: 2g | Protein: 41g

KETO EGG CUPS WITH DICED VEGETABLES

Preparation: 5 minutes | Cooking: 10 minutes | Serves: 4

Ingredients:

- Eggs - 4
- Diced vegetables (mushrooms, onions, tomatoes, bell peppers, etc.) - 1 cup
- Cheddar cheese, shredded -½ cup
- Half and Half - ¼ cup
- Salt and Pepper – as per need
- chopped cilantro - 2 tablespoons
- shredded cheese - ½ cup

Cooking directions

1. Mix up all vegetables, eggs, Half and Half, half of the cheese and pepper, salt and chopped cilantro.

2. Divide the mix into 4 wide mouth containers. (½ pint wide mouth container/jar preferable)

3. Cover it with aluminum foils.

4. Now put two cups of water in the Instant Pot, and keep a stand in the pot.

5. Put the egg pots on the stand.

6. Cook it for 5 minutes at heavy pressure.

7. Immediately discharge the pressure manually.

8. Remove the foil and top it with the remaining cheese and set your Instant Pot to warm mode until the cheese start to melt.

9. Serve hot.

Nutritional values: Calories: 115 | Total Fats: 9g | Net Carbs: 2g | Protein: 9g

KETO EGG WRAPS

Preparation: 2 minutes | Cooking: 3 minutes | Serves: 4

Ingredients:

- Eggs - 6
- Coconut oil - 1 tablespoon
- Salt/pepper to taste

Cooking directions:

1. Beat the eggs in a bowl with no lumps.

2. Set your Instant Pot to Sauté mode and press start.

3. In the insert pot, pour some coconut oil in medium heat.

4. When the pot is hot pour the mixture of egg into it and then spread the egg into a thin layer by using non-stick spatula.

5. When you are using eggs as wraps thinner coating of the egg is better for the cooking.

6. Once it cooked well on one side, flip it.

7. Place the cooked wrap on a plate and let it cool.

8. Repeat the process with every egg.

9. Put the desired filling within and roll up.

Nutritional values: Calories: 191.6 | Total Fats: 18.7g | Net Carbs: 4g | Protein 5.5g | Fiber: 1g | Sugars: 4g

KETO MUSHROOM OMELET

Preparation: 5 minutes | Cooking: 10 minutes | Serves: 1

Ingredients:

- Eggs – 3
- Butter, for frying – 1 ounce
- Shredded cheese – 1 ounce
- Yellow onion – ½
- Mushrooms – 3
- Salt to taste
- Pepper to taste

Cooking directions:

1. Take a bowl and break the eggs into it.

2. Add a pinch of salt and pepper.

3. Now, beat the eggs with a fork until it becomes smooth and bubbly.

4. Select your Instant Pot to Sauté mode and when the pot become hot, put some butter and bring to medium heat.

5. Let the butter melt and spread in the pan.

6. Pour the egg mixture into the pan.

7. When the omelet begins to harden, but is still a little raw on its top, put cheese, onion, and mushrooms over it.

8. Ease the corners of the omelet using the spatula and fold it by putting the one half of the omelet over the other half.

9. Your omelet will be ready once it starts to look brownish golden.

10. Serve it hot.

Nutritional values: Calories: 510 | Fat: 43g | Carbohydrates: 4g | Fiber: 1g | Protein: 25g

KETO SCRAMBLED EGGS WITH HALLOUMI CHEESE

Preparation: 10 minutes | Cooking: 15 minutes | Serves: 1

Ingredients:

- Halloumi cheese, diced – 1½ ounces
- Bacon, diced – 1¾ ounces
- Olive oil – 1 tablespoon
- Scallion – 1
- Eggs – 2
- Fresh parsley, chopped – 2¼ ounces
- Pitted olives – 2¼ ounces
- Salt to taste
- Pepper to taste

Cooking directions:

1. Cut halloumi cheese and bacon into small cubes.
2. Set your Instant Pot on Sauté mode and add oil in the insert pot and bring to medium temperature.
3. Sauté halloumi, scallions and bacon in it. You need to fry it until they become brown.
4. Add salt, pepper, eggs, and parsley in a small bowl and mix well.
5. Pour the mix into the sautéing pot over the cheese and bacon.
6. Continue sautéing on low medium temperature.
7. Add some olives and stir it for a few minutes.
8. Your scrambled eggs are ready.
9. You can also serve it with salad.

Nutritional values: Calories: 667 | Fat: 59g | Net Carbohydrates: 4g | Fiber: 2g | Protein: 28g

BRUSSEL SPROUT WITH BACON

Preparation: 5 minutes | Cooking: 25 minutes | Serves: 4

Ingredients:

- Brussel sprouts, chopped – 4 cups
- Bacon diced – 3 or 4 slices
- Honey – 1 tablespoon
- Salt – as required to taste
- Water - ½ cup

Cooking directions:

1. First of all, slice the bacon into small square pieces.

2. Set your Instant Pot on Sauté mode and press start.

3. Add bacon and sauté for about 6-7 minutes. Stir continuously and don't let it burn.

4. Meantime, while the bacon is cooking, you can chop the Brussel sprouts.

5. Add the chopped Brussels to the sautéing pot after 7 minutes and continue sautéing for another 5 minutes.

6. When the 5 minutes elapsed, add water.

7. Stop sautéing and close the lid of the Instant Pot.

8. Set the cooking to manual high-pressure cooking for 2 minutes.

9. After two minutes release the pressure manually.

10. Transfer the vegetables to a serving pot and sprinkle salt and honey.

11. Serve hot.

Nutritional values: Calories: 94 | Carbohydrate: 11g | Protein: 5g | Sugars: 7g | Fat: 4g

BUTTER-FRIED BROCCOLI

Preparation: 5 minutes | Cooking: 10 minutes | Serves: 4

Ingredients:

- Butter - 3 ounces
- Broccoli - 1 pound
- Scallions - 5
- Small capers (optional) - 2 tablespoons
- Salt and pepper – to taste

Cooking directions:

1. Divide the broccoli into little florets, together with the stem.

2. You should peel off the skin of the stem before coarsely chopping.

3. Now set your Instant Pot to sauté mode and add butter, then add broccoli into it.

4. Let it sauté for about 5 minutes until the broccoli becomes brown and soft.

5. Then season it with pepper and salt.

6. Finally put in some finely chopped capers and scallions.

7. Close the lid and vent.

8. Now select pressure cooker mode and cook in low pressure about 5 minutes.

9. Release pressure manually.

10. Serve hot.

Nutritional values: Calories: 202 | Total Fats: 19g | Net Carbs: 5g | Protein: 3g | Fiber: 3g

BUTTER-FRIED GREEN CABBAGE

Preparation: 5 minutes | Cooking: 15 minutes | Serves: 1

Ingredients:

- Shredded green cabbage – 0.400 pounds
- Butter – 1½ tablespoons
- Salt to taste
- Pepper to taste

Cooking directions:

1. Chop the cabbage finely with the help of a food processor. You can even use a mandolin slicer or a sharp knife.

2. Set your Instant Pot to sauté mode.

3. Add butter to it.

4. Add the cabbage and sauté. Stir it for at least fifteen minutes until the cabbage turns golden brown around the sides.

5. Add salt and pepper as per your taste.

6. Serve hot.

Nutritional values: Calories: 194 | Fat: 17g | Net Carbohydrates: 6g | Fiber: 4g | Protein: 2g

INSTANT POT KETO KALE SALAD

Preparation: 5 minutes | Cooking: 3 minutes | Serves: 4

Ingredients:

- Kale heads, rib less, chopped to small pieces – 2 large
- Olive oil, virgin - 2 tablespoons
- Pepper flakes, crushed - ⅛ teaspoon
- Water - ⅓ cup
- Lemon juice – 1 Lemon
- Salt - ¾ teaspoon

Cooking directions:

1. Wash and clean kale.

2. Remove the ribs and chop into small bite pieces.

3. Take your Instant Pot and put olive oil, red pepper, salt and chopped kale.

4. Add water.

5. Lock the lid and set to manual pressure cook for 3 minutes.

6. After 3 minutes, go for a quick pressure release.

7. Open the lid and squeeze lemon juice.

8. Mix it properly and add salt and pepper flakes if required.

9. Serve hot.

Nutritional values: Calories: 49 | Total Carbs: 8.8g | Protein: 4.3g | Fat: 0.9g | Fiber: 3.6g | Sugars: 2.3g | Sodium: 38mg

LOW-CRAB BROCCOLI MASH

Prep Time: 10 minutes | Cooking: 10 minutes | Serves: 4

Ingredients:

- Broccoli - 1½ pounds
- Fresh basil or fresh parsley, finely chopped - 4 tablespoons
- Butter - 3 ounces
- Garlic clove - 1
- Water ½ cup
- Salt and pepper – to taste

Instructions:

1. Set your Instant Pot to sauté mode.

2. After heating the pot add butter and after melting butter add garlic. Sauté for about half minute.

3. Cut the fresh broccoli into florets.

4. Then peel and slice its stem into little pieces.

5. Pour half cup water to the Instant Pot.

6. Put broccoli along with all the ingredients in the pot.

7. Close the lid and vent.

8. Set your Instant Pot to High Pressure manual for 1 minute.

9. Release the pressure manually.

10. Now mix with all other items in a food processor

11. Add salt and pepper as per taste.

12. Add little more oil or margarine or butter (if you wish).

13. Serve hot.

Nutritional values: Calories: 191 | Total Fat: 18g | Cholesterol: 46mg | Total Carbohydrate: 8g | Sodium: 279mg | Protein: 3g | Sugar: 2g

LOW-CARB CAULIFLOWER RICE

Preparation: 5 minutes | Cooking: 15 minutes | Serves: 1

Ingredients:

- Cauliflower – ½ pound
- Salt – ⅛ teaspoon
- Turmeric – ⅛ teaspoon (Optional)
- Butter or coconut oil – 1¾ tablespoon

Cooking directions:

1. With the help of a grater, chop the entire head of the cauliflower finely.

2. Set your Instant Pot to sauté mode.

3. When the pot become hot add butter or coconut.

4. Add the cauliflower in the pot and sauté it until it becomes soft.

5. Add salt and turmeric to it while frying.

6. Serve hot.

Nutritional values: Calories: 208 | Fat: 19g | Net Carbohydrates: 6g | Fiber: 4g | Protein: 4g

LOW-CARB ZUCCHINI AND WALNUT SALAD

Prep Time: 10 minutes | Cooking: 5 minutes | Serves: 4

Ingredients:

- Zucchini - 2
- Olive oil - 1 tablespoon
- Salt and pepper to taste
- Head of Romaine lettuce - 1
- Arugula lettuce - 4 ounces
- Finely chopped fresh chives or scallions - 4 tablespoons
- Chopped walnuts or pecans - ¾ cup

Cooking directions:

1. In a little bowl, mix all ingredients for the dressing.

2. Keep the dressing intact to increase the flavor of the salad.

3. Now split the zucchini along the length to scoop out all the seeds.

4. Then slice the zucchini halves corner to corner into half inch pieces.

5. Set your Instant Pot in Sauté mode and press to start on medium heat.

6. Add olive oil.

7. When the oil becomes hot, put in the slices of zucchini and sauté.

8. Season with pepper and salt.

9. Sauté it for few minutes until zucchini becomes lightly brown and firm.

10. Cut the salad.

11. Put the chives and romaine, arugula in a large bowl.

12. Stir in the mix to the pan of zucchini.

13. Then roast all the nuts for a split second in the same pan along with zucchini.

14. Season with pepper and salt.

15. Now spoon out nuts onto the salad to spot with salad dressing.

Nutritional values: Calories: 638 | Total Fat: 61g | Cholesterol: 16.6mg | Total Carbohydrate: 12g | Sodium: 1185mg | Protein: 7.9g | Sugars: 6.2g

SOUPS AND STEWS

BRAZILIAN SOPA DE PALMITO

Preparation time: 15 minutes | Cooking: 8 minutes | Serves: 4

Ingredients:

- Hearts of palm, un-drained - 1 can
- Onion, large - 1
- Chicken broth – 1½ cup
- Salt - 1 teaspoon
- Pepper - 1½ teaspoons
- Garlic, finely chopped - 2 teaspoon

For garnishing:

- Heavy cream - 3½ ounces
- Shredded parmesan - 2½ ounces
- Fresh nutmeg, grated - ½ teaspoon
- Scallions, finely chopped – 1 ounces

Cooking directions:

1. Pour the Hearts of Palm into the Instant Pot along with the liquid.

2. Now add onion, pepper, garlic, chicken broth, and salt into the pot.

3. Set the cooker to manual high pressure for 8 minutes.

4. After cooking, let it release the pressure naturally for 10 minutes and after that release the pressure manually.

5. Remove the lid and allow it to cool.

6. With the help of a blender, blend the mix to a smooth soup

7. Now stir heavy cream, parmesan cheese, and nutmeg and blend them until everything mixed well.

8. Garnish the soup with chopped scallions and serve hot.

Nutritional values: Calories: 231 | Total Fats: 20g | Net Carbs: 7g | Protein: 6g | Fiber: 1g | Cholesterol: 5mg | Sodium: 456mg | Potassium: 2,146 mg | Sugars: 2g

BROCCOLI CHEDDAR SOUP

Preparation time: 5 minutes | Cooking: 20 minutes | Serves: 6

Ingredients:

- Butter - 5 tablespoon
- Diced, yellow onion - 1
- Garlic clove, minced - 1
- Cream cheese - 1¾ ounces
- Vegetable or chicken broth - 1½ cup
- Heavy whipping cream – 7 ounces
- Broccoli florets - 1 pound
- Carrot - ½ pound
- Salt - ¾ teaspoon
- Ground black pepper - ½ teaspoon
- Smoked paprika - ½ teaspoon
- Ground mustard - 1 teaspoon
- Chipotle pepper powder - ¼ teaspoon
- Smoked cheddar cheese - 3½ ounces

Method:

1. Select your Instant Pot cooking mode to Sauté high and when the pot becomes hot, melt one tablespoon of butter.
2. Once the butter melts, add diced onion and sauté it about 4-5 minutes until they turn golden brown. Stir continuously.
3. Now add minced garlic and stir and cook it for 1 minute.
4. Now add the broth and heavy whipping cream in the pot and continue stirring in medium low temperature for about 8-10 minutes. Stir the pot occasionally to avoid sticking at the bottom.
5. After that add the remaining butter and cream cheese into the pot. Stir the mixture until it becomes thick for about 1-2 minutes.
6. After done, stop sautéing.
7. Add all the vegetables, salt, pepper, paprika, ground mustard, and chipotle pepper powder to the pot and stir it to combine everything and close the Instant Pot lid.
8. Seal the vent valve and change the cooking mode manual high pressure for 2 minute.
9. Once the cooking over, allow it to stay for 5 minutes and release the pressure manually.
10. Remove the soup from the pot to serving bowl and add cheddar cheese to the bowl.
11. Garnish with some cheddar cheese on the top, while serving.

Nutritional values: Calories: 526 | Total Fats: 49g | Net Carbs: 9g | Protein: 13g | Fiber: 2g | Cholesterol: 162mg | Sodium: 1,069mg | Potassium: 405mg | Sugars: 2g

LOW-CARB CREAMY BROCCOLI AND LEEK SOUP

Preparation: 5 minutes | Cooking: 15 minutes | Serves: 4

Ingredients:

- Leek – 1
- Broccoli – ⅔ pound
- Water – 3 cups
- Garlic – 1 clove
- Creamy cheese – 8 ounces
- Butter – 4 ounces
- Salt and pepper to taste
- Paprika powder – ½ teaspoon
- Cheese chips – 3 ounces

Cooking directions:

1. Take a bowl of water, add little rock salt and rinse both leak and broccoli for some time.
2. Drain the water and pat dry.
3. Cut the core of the broccoli into thin slices and divide into small florets.
4. Follow the same for leek too.
5. Set your Instant Pot to sauté mode and pour 1 tablespoon butter.
6. Add Leek, garlic, paprika in the pot and sauté for 5 minutes until it becomes soft.
7. Now stop sautéing.
8. Add broccoli, broccoli stems, salt, pepper, water into the Instant Pot and set to manual high pressure for 8 minutes.
9. Once done release pressure manually.
10. Now add cream cheese and remaining butter. Use a blender to bring it to the right soup consistency.
11. Add cream and cheese chips before serving. If you want to have a thin soup, add little water to it.
12. Serve hot and enjoy.

Nutritional values: Calories: 504 | Fat: 47g | Protein: 13g | Fiber: 3g | Net Carbs: 8g

CREAMY VENISON STEW

Preparation: 15 minutes | Cooking: 30 minutes | Serves: 6

Ingredients:

- Olive oil - 4 tablespoons
- Venison or chuck roast - 1¾ pounds
- Carrot, sliced - 1
- Yellow onion chopped - 1
- Garlic clove, minced - 1
- Tamari soy sauce - 1 tablespoon
- Heavy whipping cream - 1 cup
- Dried rosemary - 1 tablespoon
- Paprika powder - 1 teaspoon

- Dried juniper berries - 3
- Celery root - 1⅓ pounds
- Butter - 2 tablespoons
- Salt and ground black - pepper as required to taste

Paprika Butter preparation:

- Butter - 4 ounces
- Paprika powder - 1 teaspoon
- Salt or ground black pepper – to taste

Cooking directions:

1. In room-temperature, mix-up butter and paprika powder carefully.
2. Add some salt and pepper as per need.
3. Set the mixture to the side for later use.
4. Now cut the meat into small pieces about one inch cube size.
5. Set your Instant Pot to Sauté mode and pour half of the olive oil.
6. Brown all the meat pieces in separate batches until it is well seared.
7. Season them generously with salt and pepper.
8. When the final batch of meat cubes is going to be golden browned, remove and keep it aside.
9. Now add all the veggies excluding the celery root to the cooking pan used for the meat, and put in the remaining oil.
10. Sauté it at least for one minute or two over medium-high temperature.
11. Now place the fried meat back into the pan again.
12. Then add all leftover ingredients including paprika butter and celery root.
13. Close the lid and pressure vent.
14. Set the Instant Pot cooking mode to high pressure cook for 20 minutes.
15. After cooking allow the pressure to release naturally.
16. Serve medium hot.

Nutritional values: Calories: 598 | Total Fats: 47g | Net Carbs: 11g | Protein 32g | Fiber: 3g | Sugars: 4g

DAIRY-FREE CREAMY CHICKEN SOUP

Preparation time: 10 minutes | Cooking: 10 minutes | Serves: 2

Ingredients:

- Cauliflower florets – 1¼ pounds
- Chicken broth – 1 cup
- Unsweetened almond milk - 1 cup
- Onion powder – 1 teaspoon
- Grey sea salt – ½ teaspoon
- Garlic powder - ¼ teaspoon
- Freshly ground black pepper – ¼ teaspoon
- Celery seed (optional) – ⅛ teaspoon
- Dried thyme – ⅛ teaspoon
- Collagen Protein Beef Gelatin – ¼ cup
- Chicken thighs, cooked, sliced – ¼ cup

Cooking directions:

1. Select your Instant Pot to sauté mode.

2. Add all ingredients except cooked chicken and gelatin and sauté for about 7-8 minutes until the cauliflower florets become soft.

3. Using a spoon, transfer a ½ cup of the hot liquid to a medium-sized bowl.

4. Now, add gelatin scoop by scoop and make sure it dissolves in the liquid.

5. Blend the gelatin and cauliflower mixture by using a food processor or use an immersion blender to blend it until it becomes smooth. It will take about 2 minutes.

6. Transfer gelatin and cauliflower mixture to the Instant Pot

7. Now add the cooked chicken to the gelatin and cauliflower mixture.

8. Close the Instant Pot lid, close the pressure vent and select manual high pressure for 2 minutes.

9. Once cooking over, release the pressure manually.

10. Serve hot with sauce.

Nutritional values: Calories: 198 | Saturated Fat: 1.1g | Cholesterol: 24mg | Sodium: 672mg | Carbs: 9.4g | Dietary Fiber: 3.8g | Sugars: 3.3g | Protein: 26.4g | Total Fat: 6.9g

INSTANT POT LOW CARB TACO SOUP

Preparation time: 10 minutes | Cooking: 10 minutes | Serves: 8

Ingredients:

- Ground beef – 2¼ pounds
- Onion flakes - 1 tablespoon (optional)
- Garlic cloves, minced - 4
- Chili powder - 2 tablespoon
- Cumin - 2 teaspoons
- Tomatoes, diced - ¼ pound
- Beef broth - ½ cup
- Salt – to taste
- Pepper – to taste
- Cream Cheese - 1¾ ounces

Topping:

- Sour cream - 2 tablespoon
- Jalapeño pepper, sliced - 2
- Cheddar cheese, shredded - 2 tablespoon

Method:

1. Sauté the ground beef in the instant pot until it becomes brown and drain the excess fat liquid.

2. Stir in the onions, garlic, chili powder, and beef broth, diced tomatoes.

3. Add chili, salt and pepper.

4. Cover the instant pot and cook for 5 minutes in soup setting. It is advisable to pressure cook the soup for a shorter period and then let it sit in the bowl for a more extended period.

5. When the timer reaches 5 minutes, remove the excess pressure manually from the pot and let it settle for 10 minutes before opening the lid.

6. Add cream cheese and shredded cheddar cheese on the top.

7. Serve hot with extra toppings.

Nutritional values: Calories: 386 | Total Fats: 19g | Net Carbs: 8g | Protein: 27g | Fiber: 1g | Cholesterol: 123mg | Sodium: 831mg | Potassium: 261mg | Sugars: 4g

INSTANT POT LOW-CARB CAULIFLOWER SOUP

Preparation: 25 minutes | Cooking: 12 minutes | Serves: 6

Ingredients:

- Butter – 2 tablespoon
- Onion, finely chopped - ½ onion
- Garlic powder – 1 teaspoon
- Cream cheese cubes – 4 ounces
- Chicken stock – 3 cups

- Half and Half cream - ½ cup
- Grated cheddar cheese – 1 cup
- Kosher salt – 1 teaspoon
- Cauliflower heads, finely chopped without leaves and stem – 8 cups

For topping:

- Sour cream
- Cooked bacon strips, crumbled – 10
- Finely grated cheddar cheese
- Green onions, finely chopped

Cooking method:

1. Slice some onion for toping and set aside.
2. Set the Instant Pot to Sauté mode.
3. Sauté bacon for 3-4 minutes in low medium temperature and crumble it. Remove the bacon and keep aside.
4. Peel, clean and finely chop onions.
5. Remove the leaves and stems of cauliflower and coarsely chop it.
6. Now put butter into the Instant Pot cooker in Sauté mode.
7. Add the chopped onions and cook about 3 minutes.
8. Now put chopped cauliflower, garlic powder, chicken.
9. Put salt to taste.
10. Close the lid and vent of the cooker.
11. Cook on manual high pressure for 5 minutes.
12. Release the pressure manually.
13. When the cooking continues, you can start preparing the grated cheddar cheese, cream cheese and Half and Half.
14. Mix sour cream and grated cheese.
15. Check the tenderness of the cauliflower.
16. Transfer the mix to a food processor and puree the soup.
17. Add chicken stock, if you want to thin the consistency of the soup.
18. Add the cream cheese cubes and grated cheddar cheese.
19. Continue stirring in the food processor until it melts and mixes thoroughly.
20. Keep the Instant Pot in warm mode.
21. Transfer the soup back to the instant pot and warm the soup.
22. Add salt to taste and season it with black pepper ground.
23. Top it with chopped green onion, sour cream, grated cheese and crumbled bacon. Serve hot.

Nutritional values: Calories: 193 | Carbs: 5g | Fat: 16g | Cholesterol: 0mg | Sugars: 0g | Sodium: 450mg | Potassium: 0mg | Fiber: 3g | Protein: 6g

CAULIFLOWER SOUP WITH CRISP PANCETTA

Preparation: 10 minutes | Cooking: 10 minutes | Serves: 6

Ingredients:

- Cauliflower – 1 pound
- Chicken broth or Vegetable stock – 4 cups
- Butter – 4 ounces
- Diced bacon or pancetta – 7 ounces
- Butter – 1 tablespoon
- Smoked chili powder – 1 teaspoon
- Pecans – 3 ounces
- Salt and pepper to taste

Cooking directions:

1. Take cauliflower and divide into small florets.

2. Add salt and turmeric to the hot water and add these florets to remove any germs if any.

3. Set your Instant Pot to sauté mode, low medium heat and put butter into it.

4. When butter start to melt put the finely chopped cauliflower and sliced bacon or pancetta. Stir until cooked. It will take about 4-5 minutes.

5. Add cream and butter to it.

6. Mix with the chicken or vegetable stock and sauté for 2-3 minutes.

7. Stop sautéing and close the lid and vent.

8. Set the Instant Pot to manual high pressure for 2 minutes.

9. Wait for 10 minutes and release the pressure manually after cooking

10. Open the lid and when the temperature becomes low, mix the soup using a blender to the correct consistency

11. Add salt and pepper and chili powder to taste

12. Serve hot with sauce.

Nutritional values: Calories: 534 | Carbs: 6g | Fat: 53g | Protein: 10g

KETO CHICKEN CURRY STEW

Preparation: 10 minutes | Cooking: 16 minutes | Serves: 4

Ingredients:

- Boneless chicken thighs - 1½ pounds
- Curry powder - 2 tablespoons
- Garlic powder - 2 teaspoons
- Coconut oil - ⅓ cup
- Cauliflower - 1 pound
- Green bell pepper - 1
- Coconut milk - 14 ounces
- Salt and pepper – to taste
- Fresh cilantro or fresh parsley - 4 tablespoons

Cooking directions:

1. At first, cut the chicken into small pieces.

2. Slice the peppers and cauliflower into pieces.

3. Now heat up coconut oil in Sauté mode in your Instant Pot on medium low heat.

4. Add some minced garlic and curry powder and sauté it for a minute until it releases the flavors.

5. At this junction add chicken and season it with salt and pepper.

6. Sauté it for about 5 minutes in low medium heat.

7. Stir repeatedly to make sure that all pieces are made golden brown and carefully cooked through.

8. Now add bell pepper, and cauliflower to the same pan.

9. Sauté all the veggies on medium-high heat for 5 minutes.

10. Then add the coconut milk and fried chicken into it.

11. Now close the lid and close the pressure vent.

12. Set your Instant Pot to manual high pressure for 5 minutes.

13. When the cooking over, wait for 10 minutes and release the pressure manually.

14. Open the lid and add salt and pepper for seasoning.

15. Finally, serve the dish with finely chopped cilantro scattered on top.

Nutritional values: Calories: 781 | Total Fats: 68g | Net Carbs: 9g | Protein: 33g | Fiber: 5g

KETO VEGETABLE SOUP WITH FENNEL AND CELERY ROOT

Preparation: 5 minutes | Cooking: 15 minutes | Serves: 4

Ingredients:

- Olive oil – 2 tablespoons
- Finely chopped celery root - ½ pound
- Fennel - ⅔ pounds
- Garlic – 1 full clove
- Coriander seeds – 1 teaspoon
- Water – 3½ cups
- Butter – Adequate
- Vegetable bouillon cube - 1
- Ground nutmeg – ¼ teaspoon
- Lemon Juice – Finely squeezed
- Salt & Black pepper to taste
- Freshly chopped cilantro – handful

Cooking directions:

1. Rinse fennel, cilantro and celery roots in fresh water and chop it finely.

2. In your Instant Pot, select sauté mode and pour little oil.

3. When the oil become hot, sauté the vegetable on high medium heat about 4-5 minutes, until it become soft.

4. Add coriander seeds and nutmeg, stir for a minute.

5. Stop sautéing and add water and vegetable bouillon cube.

6. Close the lid and vents.

7. Select manual high pressure cooker mode for 5 minutes.

8. After cooking allow it to release the pressure manually for 5 minutes.

9. Then release the remaining pressure manually.

10. Again select sauté mode and add butter and stir it slowly until the butter melts. It will take about 4 minutes.

11. Stop sautéing and add lemon juice otherwise it tastes bitter.

12. Add salt and pepper for your taste.

13. Garnish with finely chopped cilantro and celery roots.

14. As an additional topping, you may add cooked chicken or cheese with toasted nuts and serve hot with sauce.

Nutritional values: Calories: 371 | Net Carbs: 9g | Fat: 36g | Protein: 2g | Fiber: 4g

LOW CARB BEEF STEW

Preparation: 20 minutes | Cooking: 50 minutes | Serves: 6

Ingredients:

- Beef chuck roast, cubed – 1¼ pounds
- Mushroom whole – ½ pound
- Celery root, peeled & ¾ inch cubed – ½ cup
- Pearl onions, trimmed & peeled) – 1
- Celery ribs sliced – 2 to 3
- Carrot roll-cut – ½ cup
- Garlic fresh sliced – 2 cloves
- Tomato paste – 2 teaspoons
- Olive oil/avocado oil or bacon grease – 2 teaspoons
- Beef broth – 5 cups
- Bay leaf large – 1
- Thyme dried – ½ teaspoon
- Salt – to taste

Cooking directions:

1. In your Instant Pot, select Sauté mode.
2. When the pot is hot enough, pour oil and spread in the bottom well.
3. Put mushrooms into the pot and stir occasionally on medium high heat for 4 minutes.
4. Remove the mushroom and put the other vegetables and sauté for 2 minutes.
5. Remove the cooked vegetables.
6. Brown the meat in sauté mode in batches by adding more oil as required. It will take about 6-8 minutes.
7. Now put the bay leaf, tomato paste, thyme and make sure to coat the beef with these ingredients. Stir it continuously.
8. Let it cook for about a minute and add the broth in batches while you continue to stir the pot.
9. Add all the cooked vegetables.
10. Cover the lid and close the vent.
11. Set the Instant Pot, manual pressure cook for 35 minutes.
12. Once the cooking over, allow it to release the entire pressure naturally.
13. Open the lid and check the tenderness of the meat.
14. If the meat is not tender, then pressure cook it for another 10 minutes.
15. Add the salt and pepper as required and add spices as well if needed.
16. Serve hot.

Nutritional values: Calories: 288 | Total Fats: 20g | Net Carbs: 8g | Protein: 20g | Fiber: 8g | Cholesterol: 240mg | Sodium: 58mg | Potassium: 0mg | Sugars: 0g

LOW CARB BUFFALO CHICKEN SOUP

Preparation: 30 minutes | Cooking: 18 minutes | Serves: 6

Ingredients:

- Deli-roasted chicken, skinned, boned & coarsely shredded – 2½ pounds
- Butter unsalted – 2 teaspoons
- Celery coarsely chopped – ½ cup
- Onion chopped – ½ cup
- Sodium chicken broth – 2 cup
- Skimmed milk – 1½ cup
- Hot pepper sauce – 1 teaspoon
- Mozzarella cheese – 1½ cups
- Crumbled blue cheese – 1 ¼ cups
- Shredded parmesan cheese – ½ cup
- Xanthan gum – ¾ teaspoon

Cooking directions:

1. Set your Instant Pot to Sauté mode medium heat.
2. Add butter and heat to melt for 2 minutes.
3. Add celery and onion.
4. Sauté until it becomes translucent for 4-5 minutes in medium heat.
5. Pour broth, milk and one tablespoon of pepper sauce and keep stirring the mixture for 3-4 minutes.
6. In another bowl add some mozzarella, blue cheese, parmesan and xanthan gum as per the given measurement and add this mix to the soup gradually while you continue to stir the soup.
7. Stir until the cheese melts well for 3 minutes.
8. Stop sautéing.
9. Add ¾ of the roasted chicken
10. Close the lid and vent.
11. Set the Instant Pot manual high pressure cook for 4 minutes.
12. Allow it release the pressure naturally for 10 minutes.
13. Release the remaining pressure manually.
14. Put the remaining chicken on top of it.
15. Top it with hot sauce, and blue cheese.
16. Serve hot.

Nutritional values: Calories: 478.2 | Total Fats: 23.6g | Net Carbs: 7.5g | Protein: 56.6g | Fiber: 8g | Cholesterol: 157.1mg | Sodium: 1,779mg | Potassium: 0mg | Sugars: 0g

LOW CARB CAULIFLOWER SOUP WITH BACON AND CHEESE

Preparation Time: 15 minutes | Cooking: 20 minutes | Serves: 5

Ingredients:

- Cauliflower, only floral portion - 1
- Carrots - ⅓ cup
- Celery – 1 cup
- Chicken stock – 1 can (32 ounces)
- Cloves garlic – 2 large
- Heavy cream - ¾ cup
- Bacon – 3 slices
- Stick of butter - ½
- Cheddar cheese – 1 cup
- Parmesan for garnish - ½ cup

Instructions:

1. Chop veggies and put aside.
2. Finely cut half portion of the cauliflower and grind the other half
3. Sauté bacon in the Instant Pot until it becomes crisp and keep aside.
4. Now into the bacon fat add butter.
5. Add the grounded cauliflower to the pan so that it will thicken the soup.
6. Add all the remaining veggies and cauliflower and sauté for around 5 minutes.
7. Pour in cream and combine.
8. Add garlic, salt, and pepper.
9. Pour in chicken stock and set Instant Pot to manual high pressure cook for 15 minutes.
10. After 15 minutes allow it to release the pressure naturally.
11. Open the lid and add cheddar cheese and mix it thoroughly.
12. Now add bacon to the soup.
13. Serve hot.

Nutritional values: Calories: 462 | Fats: 37g | Proteins: 22g | Carbohydrates: 8g

OLD FASHIONED BEEF STEW

Preparation: 15 minutes | Cooking: 45 minutes | Serves: 4

Ingredients:

- Chuck roast - ⅓ pounds
- Butter or olive oil – 2 ounces
- Yellow onion - 1
- Garlic cloves - 2
- Red wine, dry - ⅓ cup
- Water - ¾ cup

- Meat bouillon cube - 1
- Bay leaf - 1
- Dried rosemary - ½ teaspoon
- Dried thyme - ½ teaspoon
- Carrot - 1
- Celery stalks - 4 ounces

Cauliflower Mash:

- Cauliflower - 1¾ pounds
- Butter or olive oil - 3 ounces
- Ground nutmeg - ⅛ teaspoon
- Salt and ground black pepper to taste

Cooking directions:

1. First prepare the cauliflower mash.
2. Cut the cauliflower and rinse gently. If you wish, you can use the leaves and stems too by cutting into small pieces.
3. Set the Instant Pot to Sauté mode.
4. Pour two cup water and parboil it in slightly salted water for 5 minutes until it becomes soft.
5. Drain water and put in a bowl.
6. Now add butter and with an immersion blender, mash the cauliflower to the preferred consistency.
7. Keep it aside after seasoning with pepper, salt and nutmeg.
8. Now, cut the chuck roast into one inch small cubes.
9. Clean the Instant Pot, and in Sauté mode brown the meat in separate batches over medium high temperature for 6-8 minutes.
10. Season with salt and pepper.
11. Now chop up garlic and onion finely to add to the pot.
12. Lower the temperature to low medium and cook it for 2-3 minutes.
13. Now add wine, bouillon cube, water, bay leaf, thyme, and rosemary.
14. Cut carrot and celery leaves and put into the stew.
15. Close the cooker cover and change to pressure cook mode.
16. Set manual high pressure cook for 30 minutes.
17. After cooking allow it release the pressure naturally.
18. Transfer the stew to a serving bowl.
19. Serve cauliflower mash beside the stew on a serving dish.

Nutritional values: Calories: 619 | Total Fats: 47g | Net Carbs: 11g | Protein 34g | Fiber: 5g

WILD MUSHROOM SOUP

Preparation: 10 minutes | Cooking: 15 minutes | Serves: 4

Ingredients:

- Shallot – 1
- Oyster mushrooms, big - 5
- Garlic – 1 clove
- Water – 3 cups
- Dried thyme – ½ teaspoon
- Heavy cream – 1 cup
- Celery root – ½ pound
- Chicken cube or vegetable cube – 1
- Butter – 4 ounces
- White Vinegar – 1 tablespoon
- Fresh finely chopped parsley

Cooking directions:

1. Wash Mushrooms and celery roots in water and chop them.

2. Set the Instant Pot to Sauté mode.

3. Add butter, and sauté chopped vegetables over medium high temperature for 3-4 minutes.

4. To this, add thyme powder, vinegar, vegetable or chicken cube and water.

5. Stop sautéing.

6. Close the Instant Pot lid and vent.

7. Set the Instant Pot to manual, high pressure cook for 8 minutes.

8. Once the cooking over, allow it to release the pressure naturally for 10 minutes and after that release the pressure manually.

9. Open the lid and add the cream and mix with a blender.

10. Serve with finely chopped parsley.

Nutritional values: Calories: 468 | Net Carbs: 11g | Fat: 45g | Protein: 6g

SEAFOOD AND POULTRY

INSTANT POT BUTTERED COD IN SKILLET

Preparation time: 5 minutes | Cooking: 5 minutes | Serves: 2-4

Ingredients:

- Fresh or Frozen cod - 1½ pounds.
- Unsalted butter, sliced - 6 tablespoon.

For seasoning:

- Garlic powder - ¼ teaspoon
- Ground pepper - ¼ teaspoon
- Paprika - ¾ teaspoon
- Parsley or cilantro - to garnish
- Lemon, sliced – to taste
- Salt - as per taste

Instructions:

1. In a glass bowl, stir and mix well the ingredients for seasoning.

2. Put cod cut into small piece and spread the season all over evenly.

3. In the insert pot of your Instant Pot, pour two tablespoons of butter.

4. Set the Instant Pot to Sauté mode and press start and bring to medium heat.

5. When the butter becomes hot, add cod to it and cook for 2 minutes.

6. Flip cod and top with remaining butter and cook for another 5 minutes. Don't overcook; otherwise, it will become mushy and fall apart.

7. Drizzle fresh lemon juice over cod after it cooked thoroughly.

8. Serve hot immediately.

Nutritional values: Calories: 201 | Fat: 7.1g | Carbs: 1.8g | Sodium: 1mg | Fiber: 8g | Protein: 32.1g | Calcium: 0mg | Glucose: 2g

CREAMY BACON PRAWNS

Preparation time: 10 minutes | Cooking: 20 minutes | Serves: 2

Ingredients:

- Prawns - 4 ounces
- Mushrooms, sliced - 1 cup
- Bacon, nitrate free - 4 slices
- Heavy whipping cream - 1 cup
- Thyme, chopped - 1 teaspoon
- Chilly, chopped - 1 teaspoon
- Black pepper freshly ground - to taste
- Sea salt - to taste

Instructions:

1. Cut the bacon into one-inch pieces each.

2. Take your Instant Pot and set it on Sauté mode and bring to medium heat.

3. Put bacon and cook for about 5 minutes. Do not make it crispy.

4. Add sliced mushrooms to it and cook for five mins. Stir regularly.

5. Now add prawns and sauté on medium high heat for 2 minutes

6. Then add cream, chilly, thyme, pepper, and salt. Cook it for about one minute on low heat until cream becomes thick.

7. Serve hot and enjoy with family.

Nutritional values: Calories: 559 | Total Fats: 52g | Net Carbs: 5g | Protein: 21g | Fiber: 4g | Sodium: 431mg | Potassium: 402mg

FISH CURRY WITH COCONUT AND SPINACH

Preparation time: 5 minutes | Cooking: 20 minutes | Serves: 6

Ingredients:

- Firm white fish, cut into cubes - 2¼ pounds
- Coconut oil – 1 tablespoon
- Curry paste, any type - 2-4 tablespoons
- Coconut cream - 1¾ cup
- Water - 1½ cup
- Spinach, sliced – 4 cups

Instructions:

1. In the Instant Pot pour coconut oil and select Sauté mode.
2. Add the curry paste and cook in medium heat for 3 minutes.
3. Add water and coconut cream and bring it to boil
4. Now add fish pieces and stop sautéing.
5. Close the lid and set the Instant Pot to high pressure cooking for 7 minutes.
6. Once the cooking over, do a quick manual pressure release.
7. Open the lid and add spinach.
8. Again select sauté mode cook for another 5 minutes or until it wilts.
9. Serve hot.

Nutritional values: Calories: 314 | Total Fats: 18.5g | Net Carbs: 5.8g | Protein: 33.4g | Fiber: 2.2g

FISHERMAN'S CHOWDER

Preparation: 20 minutes | Cooking: 55 minutes | Serves: 2

Ingredients:

- Bacon, diced - 5 pieces
- Yellow onion, diced - 1
- Butter - 4 tablespoons
- Cloves garlic, minced - 4
- White wine - ¼ cup
- Paprika - 1 teaspoon
- Dried thyme - 1 teaspoon
- Chicken stock - 3 cups
- Cauliflower, core removed and finely chopped - 1 head
- Heavy cream - 2 cups
- Flaky fish like halibut or cod, shredded, cooked white - 1 pound
- Lemon juice - 1 teaspoon
- Tabasco - 1 teaspoon
- Salt and pepper to taste
- Sharp cheddar cheese, shredded - ½ cup
- Parmesan cheese, grated - 1 cup

Cooking directions:

1. In the Instant Pot, select Sauté and fry bacon on medium low heat for about 10 minutes, by stirring often until it become crisp.

2. Then add the onion and butter at this stage and increase the temperature to medium-high and continue frying for about 5 minutes.

3. Now add the garlic and fry it for another 5 minutes until onion becomes soft.

4. It is time to add white wine and continuously stir for 1 minute.

5. Add the thyme, paprika, chicken stock and cauliflower.

6. Stop the sauté mode and close the lid.

7. Now change the cooking mode the manual low pressure cooking for 8 minutes.

8. Once the cooking over, remove the pressure manually.

9. Open the lid and add the heavy cream and continue cooking in sauté mode for 10 minutes.

10. Mix the soup with an immersion blender or puree in a mixer and transfer back to the pot at low temperature.

11. Whip in the frayed fish and the rest of the items.

12. Now adjust seasoning as per need.

Nutritional values: Calories: 532 | Total Fats: 44g | Net Carbs: 9g | Protein: 23g | Fiber: 2g

LOW CARB CHIPOTLE FISH TACOS

Preparation time: 5 minutes | Cooking: 15 minutes | Serves: 4

Ingredients:

- Olive oil - 2 tablespoons
- Small Yellow onion, diced - ½ onion
- Fresh Jalapeno, chopped - 1
- Garlic pressed - 2 cloves
- Chipotle peppers in adobo sauce - 4 ounces
- Butter - 2 tablespoons
- Mayonnaise - 2 tablespoons
- Haddock fillets - 1 pound
- Tortillas, low card - 4

Instructions:

1. In your Instant Pot, heat oil and fry the diced onion until translucent for five minutes.

2. Reduce the heat to medium and add garlic, jalapeno and stir for another 2 minutes.

3. Chop the chipotles and add it to the pan along with adobo sauce.

4. Now add butter, mayonnaise and fish filets to the pan.

5. Mix everything gently well and cook for 8 minutes till the fish cooked thoroughly.

6. For making the taco shells, sauté tortillas on high heat for two minutes and shape them up to the desired shape once they cooked.

7. Fill the taco shells with the fish mix and the taco shells are ready.

8. Serve it hot.

Nutritional values: Calories: 300 | Total Fat: 20g | Carbohydrates: 7g | Protein: 24g

PAN-SEARED SALMON WITH LEMON DILL SAUCE

Preparation: 5 minutes | Cooking: 10 minutes | Serves: 4

Ingredients:

- Salmon fillets - 4 ounce
- Coconut oil - 2 tablespoons
- Salt -1 tablespoon
- Black pepper - ½ teaspoon
- Garlic powder - 1 teaspoon
- Onion powder - 1 teaspoon
- Butter - 4 tablespoons
- Greek yogurt - ½ cup
- Sour cream - ½ cup
- Olive oil - 2 tablespoons
- Dried dill - 1 tablespoon
- Lemon juice - 1 tablespoon
- Dash of Tabasco

Cooking directions:

1. Mix up all the ingredients like pepper, onion powder, salt, garlic powder together in a large bowl.

2. Sprinkle the mixture abundantly over the salmon fish and then lightly pat it in.

3. Preserve the remaining seasoning.

4. Now in your Instant Pot, heat coconut oil at medium-high temperature in sauté mode for about 2 minutes.

5. Put the salmon to the heating pan and heat the salmon fillets for about 5-6 minutes until it cooked very well on both sides.

6. Remove from Instant Pot and keep in a plate for another 2 minutes allowing it to cook from first to last.

7. The fish should be crumbled with a fork when serving.

8. Now top the fish fillets with 1 tablespoon of butter and let it soften while adding your sauce together.

9. Add the remaining items of seasoning to the sour cream and Greek yogurt.

10. Before serving, top it with a spoon of dill sauce.

Nutritional values: Calories: 558 | Total Fats: 58g | Net Carbs: 3g | Protein: 24g | Fiber: 0g

SALMON WITH BACON TOMATO CREAM SAUCE

Preparation time: 10 minutes | Cooking: 15 minutes | Serves: 2

Ingredients:

- Keta salmon filets: 6 ounces

For sauce preparation:

- Diced bacon - 2 slices
- Olive oil – 1 teaspoon
- Garlic, sliced – 1 cloves
- Onion, sliced (about 1/4 of a medium onion) - 1 ounce
- Vodka - ¼ cup
- Tomato paste – 1 teaspoon
- Heavy cream - 2 ounces
- Vodka – 1 tablespoon
- Basil - 10 leaves
- Lemon zest, grated - ½ teaspoon
- Salt and pepper to taste
- Water - 1 ounce

Instructions:

1. Set your Instant Pot on sauté mode.
2. When the insert pot become hot, add one teaspoon of olive oil.
3. Put bacon and fry for 2 minutes until it becomes crisp and brown.
4. Now add salted salmon fillets to the same pan and cook undisturbed for 4 minutes on both sides.
5. Remove the salmon from the pan and prepare the sauce.
6. Keep the sautéing to low and add garlic and onion until it softness.
7. Add vodka and heat it to reduce to half.
8. Add tomato paste and allow it to cook and then add heavy cream and water. Keep the required consistency.
9. Add one tablespoon of vodka and lemon zest. Stir the sauce till the smell of alcohol goes off.
10. Add basil and a pinch of salt and pepper. Stop sautéing.
11. Place the salmon fillets on plate and top with half of the sauce.
12. Garnish with basil.

Nutritional values: Calories: 431 | Total Fat: 19g | Carbohydrates: 6g | Fiber: 2g | Protein: 38g

ZINGY LEMON FISH

Preparation: 10 minutes | Cooking: 20 minutes | Serves: 2

Ingredients:

- Fresh Gurnard fish fillets - 7 ounces
- Butter - 3 tablespoons
- Lemon juice - 1 tablespoon
- Fine almond flour - ¼ cup
- Dried dill - 1 teaspoon
- Dried chives - 1 teaspoon
- Onion powder - 1 teaspoon
- Garlic powder - ½ teaspoon
- Salt and pepper to taste

Cooking method:

1. In a large bowl mix all the ingredients like almond flour, chives, dill, garlic powder, onion powder, salt, and pepper to spread evenly.
2. Now taking a fish fillets, press it into the flour mixture and turn to repeat.
3. The mix should cover the fillets thoroughly.
4. Place it on a separate platter when you finish the mixture pressing.
5. You can make this process beforehand and keep in the fridge until cooking.
6. Now in your Instant Pot, select sauté mode and heat half butter and half the lemon juice over medium-high temperature.
7. Here you want the butter-lemon mixture hot enough to coat the flour mix. But you should not burn the butter or turn the lime juice bitter.
8. Now cook the fish for 3 minutes, so that the fish absorb all the lemony butter.
9. Don't let the pan to become dry.
10. Now add extra lemon juice or butter if required.
11. Add other half of the butter and lemon liquid into the Instant Pot to cook the fish for an extra 3 minutes.
12. The outside layer of fish should be golden brown and nice
13. With a fork check the condition of the cooked fish. If the cooking is clear, stop sautéing and take out from the pan.
14. The fish will continue cooking when it is kept hot outside so that we can keep it away from overcooking.
15. Serve the fish fillet with steamed vegetables.

Nutrition Facts: Calories: 406 | Total Fats: 30.33g | Net Carbs: 3.55g | Protein: 29.07g | Fiber: 1.8g

CHICKEN CACCIATORE

Preparation: 5 minutes | Cooking: 30 minutes | Serves: 4

Ingredients:

- Chicken thighs with bone, skin removed – 4
- Kosher salt – 1 teaspoon
- Pepper, fresh – 1 teaspoon
- Olive oil – 1 teaspoon
- Tomatoes, crushed - 14oz approximately
- Fresh onion, diced – ½ cup
- Red bell pepper, diced – ¼ cup
- Green bell pepper, diced – ½ cup
- Oregano, dried – ½ teaspoon
- Bay leaf – 1
- Basil, chopped – 1 tablespoon (for topping)
- Parsley – 1 tablespoon (for topping)

Cooking directions:

1. Rub the chicken piece with salt and pepper as per the given measurement. Cover all the sides of the chicken to let the spice get absorbed.

2. Use an instant pot and keep the settings to 'Sauté' and sprinkle some olive oil into the pan.

3. When the pot become hot, put the chicken and brown both side of the chicken and keep it aside.

4. Spray a little more of the oil in the pot and add the onions, peppers and sauté the vegetable until it becomes soft and turn golden. It'll take about 5 minutes.

5. Once the vegetables cooked well, put the chicken into the pot, and pour the tomato puree over the vegetable and chicken.

6. Add bay leaves, oregano, and pepper.

7. Put salt to taste and stir gently.

8. Cover the lid of the pot and let the flavor absorb well.

9. Cook the chicken for approximately 25 minutes at manual high pressure and let it release the pressure naturally.

10. Remove the bay leaf from the chicken and garnish the dish with pasta and serve hot.

Nutritional values: Calories: 133 | Total Fats: 3g | Net Carbs: 10.5g | Protein: 14g | Fiber: 1g | Cholesterol: 57mg | Sodium: 273mg | Potassium: 0mg | Sugars: 5g

INSTANT POT LEMON GARLIC CHICKEN

Preparation: 5 minutes | Cooking: 30 minutes | Serves: 4

Ingredients:

- Chicken breast or chicken thigh – 2 pounds
- Sea salt – 1 teaspoon
- Onion diced – 1
- Avocado oil/ghee or lard – 1 tablespoon
- Garlic minced – 5 cloves
- Organic or homemade chicken broth – ½ cup
- Parsley dried – 1 teaspoon
- Paprika – ¼ teaspoon
- White cooking wine – ¼ cup
- Lemon juice – 1 cup
- Arrowroot flour – 3-4 teaspoons

Cooking directions:

1. Keep your Instant Pot to 'sauté' mode.

2. Add oil and when the pot becomes hot, add the diced onion and let it cook well.

3. Cook the onions for about 5-10 minutes or until it becomes soft.

4. Add the other ingredients like sea salt, avocado, garlic, chicken broth, parsley, paprika, white cooking wine, lemon juice as per the measurements.

5. Secure the lid after adding chicken as the last ingredient.

6. Close the lid and vent.

7. Keep the setting at 'Poultry' mode or cook manually for 12-15 minutes if you don't have a poultry setting.

8. Once cooked, let the steam release naturally.

9. Open the cover and add the arrowroot flour in the sauce to thicken the sauce.

10. Stir well and serve it hot.

11. You can also reheat the leftovers for later use and serve accordingly.

Nutritional values: Calories: 820 | Total Fats: 20g | Net Carbs: 4.4g | Protein: 140g | Fiber: 8g | Cholesterol: 391.6mg | Sodium: 1,532mg | Potassium: 1,624mg | Sugars: 0g

INSTANT POT BUTTER CHICKEN CURRY

Preparation Time: 5 minutes | Cooking: 14 minutes | Serving: 6 to 8

Ingredients:

- Chicken thighs, boneless skinless, cut into small pieces – 2 pounds
- Butter (or ghee) – 4 tablespoons
- Onion, peeled and chopped – 1 large
- Garlic cloves, minced – 8-10
- Freshly grated ginger – 2 tablespoons
- Curry powder – 1 tablespoon
- Garam masala – 2 teaspoons
- Smoked paprika - ¾ teaspoon
- Tomato sauce – 15 ounces
- Heavy cream – 1 cup
- Chopped cilantro for garnish
- Salt – 1 teaspoon

Instructions:

1. Put the spread, slashed onions, garlic, ginger, and all flavors in the Instant Pot.
2. Set on Sauté for 5 minutes. Blend and sauté until the onion becomes soft.
3. Add the tomato sauce and chopped chicken pieces.
4. Close the lid of the Instant Pot and set the high-pressure cooking for 7 minutes.
5. Once cooking over, using the quick release option, discharge the pressure.
6. Allow it settle for some time and open the pot.
7. Stir in the substantial cream.
8. Again set cooker to sauté mode and sauté for 2 minutes until the sauce becomes thick.
9. Garnish with cleaved cilantro.
10. Serve hot along with your favorite basmati rice.

Nutritional values: Calories: 351 | Fats: 20.1g | Proteins: 34.5g | Carbohydrates: 7.6g

INSTANT POT CHICKEN ENCHILADA BOWL

Preparation: 5 minutes | Cooking: 20 minutes | Serves: 6

Ingredients:

- Chicken breast (1 pound each) – 3
- Vegetable oil – 1 tablespoon
- Red enchilada sauce – ¾ cups
- Water – ¼ cup
- Onion – ¼ cup
- Green chilies – 14oz or ½ cup
- Cauliflower rice, steam bag – 1 cup
- Toppings – as per required like Avocado, jalapeno, Roma tomatoes & cheese.
- Seasoning – as per taste.

Cooking directions:

1. Set your Instant Pot to Sauté mode and pour one tablespoon oil.

2. Over medium heat, cook the chicken breast until it turns light brown.

3. Add the enchilada sauce, onions, chilies, water and sauté in low heat for 2-3 minutes.

4. Stop sautéing.

5. Cover the lid of the Instant Pot and set manual high pressure cook for 10 minutes.

6. After finish cooking, let the pressure release naturally for 10 minutes. Then release pressure manually.

7. Remove the chicken to a bowl and shred the chicken by using two forks as per the desired thickness and keep it aside.

8. Now set the Instant Pot to Sauté mode again and add the chicken back into the sauce and sauté for a while until it soaks up the flavor, let it sauté for 10 minutes or more until you see the sauce getting soaked up by the chicken.

9. Prepare the cauliflower rice as per the instruction on the bag and add the desired seasoning for it.

10. Top the rice with the chicken, avocado, cheese or preferred topping and serve the dish while warm.

Nutritional values: Calories: 120 | Total Fats: 2g | Net Carbs: 6g | Protein: 18g | Fiber: 1g | Cholesterol: 52mg | Sodium: 56mg | Potassium: 0mg | Sugars: 0g

INSTANT POT GARLIC BUTTER CHICKEN

Preparation: 5 minutes | Cooking: 40 minutes | Serves: 4

Ingredients:

- Chicken breasts, whole or chopped – 4
- Turmeric ghee (or regular ghee with 1 teaspoon turmeric added in the same, as per availability) – ¼ cup
- Salt – 1 teaspoon
- Garlic, peeled & diced – 10 cloves

Cooking directions:

1. Put the whole or chopped chicken breasts in the Instant Pot.

2. Now, you must add the ghee (turmeric ghee or regular ghee with the hint of turmeric approximately one teaspoon) in the pot along with the rest of the ingredient like salt and the freshly diced garlic cloves into the cooking pot.

3. Close the lid and pressure valve.

4. Set the pressure manual high for about 35 minutes.

5. As per the instructions of the pressure cooker, release the pressure to eliminate the additional steam.

6. Take the chicken pieces out.

7. Shred the chicken as per the requirement of thickness and serve it in a bowl with additional ghee if required.

Nutritional values: Calories: 404 | Total Fats: 21g | Net Carbs: 3g | Protein: 47g | Fiber: 0g | Cholesterol: 0mg | Sodium: 20mg | Potassium: 0mg | Sugars: 0g

INSTANT POT JAMAICAN CHICKEN CURRY

Preparation: 10 minutes | Cooking: 20 minutes | Serves: 4

Ingredients:

- Oil – 2 tablespoons
- Ginger, minced – 1 tablespoon
- Garlic, minced – 1 tablespoon
- Onion, chopped – 1 cup
- Jamaican curry powder – ½ tablespoon
- Scotch bonnet pepper, sliced – 1
- Thyme, springs fresh – 3
- Salt – 1 tablespoon
- Allspice ground – ½ teaspoon
- Boneless and skinless chicken thighs – 1 pound
- Potato large, cut into 1-inch cubes – 1
- Water – 1 cup

Cooking directions:

1. Let us cook it using Instant Pot. Heat the Instant Pot on 'sauté' mode and add oil once the pot turns hot enough.

2. Add some ginger and garlic as per the measurement and stir for about 2 minutes.

3. Add the onions and stir for around 1-2 minutes.

4. Now, add the Jamaican curry powder into the pot and also add the sliced scotch bonnet pepper, thyme, all spices, and salt. Stir until the mixture transforms to a good paste.

5. When the mixture turned to a thick paste, add ¼ cup of water into the pot to make it semi-liquid.

6. Finally, add the chicken, potato, and 1 cup of water into the pot and stir well.

7. Close the lid and vent.

8. Set the Instant Pot to manual high pressure cook for 7 minutes. In case if you are not using potato, you can reduce the quantity of water to half.

9. Once the cooking is over, allow it to settle for 10 minutes and after 10 minutes manually release the pressure.

10. Serve warm.

Nutritional values: Calories: 248 | Total Fats: 11g | Net Carbs: 4g | Protein: 23g | Fiber: 8g | Cholesterol: 158mg | Sodium: 72mg | Potassium: 0mg | Sugar: 0g

INSTANT POT KETO CRACK CHICKEN

Preparation Time: 15 minutes | Cooking: 30minutes | Serves: 4

Ingredients:

- Chicken breasts or chicken tenders, boneless or skinless – 2 pounds
- Creamy cheese – 12 ounces
- Dry Ranch Seasoning mix - 4 tablespoons
- Bacon crumbles – 8 ounces
- Cheddar Cheese - ½ cup
- Bone broth or water – 1 cup

Instructions:

1. Pour one cup of water or bone broth in the Instant Pot.
2. Prepare the cream cheese by cutting them into large cubes.
3. Put the chicken in the Instant Pot.
4. Add the cream cheese and the seasonings on the top of the chicken.
5. Close the lid and vent of the Instant Pot.
6. Set cooking to manual high pressure 10 minutes. Keep the pressure timer to 12 minutes if you are using chicken breasts.
7. After the set time elapsed, release the pressure manually.
8. Carefully take out the chicken in a bowl and keep the liquid for later use.
9. Shred the chicken by using two forks.
10. Place the shredded chicken back in the liquid kept in the pressure cooker.
11. Add all the cheddar cheese, and the bacon crumbles inside the shredded chicken and then mix all the ingredients.
12. Place back the lid on the pressure cooker and cook for about 5 minutes. Let the ingredients sit for a few minutes which will allow the sauce to thicken.
13. Serve and enjoy.

Nutritional values: Calories: 440 | Fats: 28.4g | Proteins: 41.4g | Carbohydrates: 3.5g

INSTANT POT WHOLE CHICKEN

Preparation Time: 5 minutes | Cooking: 33 minutes | Serving: 5

Ingredients:

- Paprika – 1 teaspoon
- Minced garlic – 1 teaspoon
- Minced ginger – 1 teaspoon
- Ground coriander – 1 teaspoon
- Mixed herbs (Herbs de Provence) – 1 teaspoon
- Ground nutmeg - ¼ teaspoon
- Salt – to taste
- Ground black pepper - ½ teaspoon
- Oil divided – 3 tablespoons
- Chicken stock divided - 1 cup (Half cup if using 6qt Instant Pot)
- Whole chicken giblets removed, washed and patted dry – 4 pounds

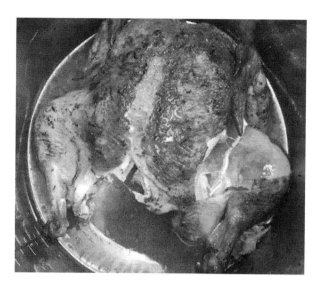

Instructions:

1. In a medium bowl combine garlic, paprika, ginger, nutmeg, coriander, pepper, herbs, salt, along with two tablespoon olive oil and two tablespoon chicken stock to make a paste.

2. Put the chicken in the same bowl and rub the paste all over the chicken and inside the chicken.

3. In the Instant Pot, select the sauté setting, and pour the remaining oil and brown the entire chicken on both sides, approximately 4 minutes each side.

4. Remove the chicken from the Instant Pot, and put aside on a plate.

5. Add the remaining chicken stock into the pot, and rub any bits stay attached to the base of the pot from browning with a wooden spoon.

6. Put a trivet in the Instant Pot to place the chicken.

7. Cover the Instant Pot and close pressure valve.

8. Select manual high-pressure cooking for 25 minutes.

9. Once the cooking over, let the steam discharge by default.

10. Let the chicken rest for 10 minutes before serving.

Nutritional values: Calories: 460 | Fats: 34g | Proteins: 32g | Carbohydrates: 2g

INSTANT POT BRUSCHETTA CHICKEN

Preparation Time: 10 minutes | Cooking: 7 minutes | Serving: 6

Ingredients:

- Chicken breasts, boneless – 2 pounds
- Chicken broth - ½ cup
- Olive oil – 1 tablespoon
- Pepper - ½ teaspoon
- Salt – to taste

Tomato Sauce:

- Diced tomatoes – 15 ounces
- Clove garlic – 4
- Dried oregano – 1 teaspoon
- Balsamic vinegar - ¼ cup
- Dried basil – 1 teaspoon

Instructions:

1. Prepare the tomato sauce by combining all the ingredients in a bowl and keep aside.
2. Cut the chicken into 6-8 tenders.
3. Now take your instant pot and set to sauté mode.
4. When the pan becomes hot, add olive oil.
5. Put the chicken in the sauté pan and sear it for half minutes.
6. After thirty minutes, just flip it and continue searing for another half minute.
7. Transfer the seared chicken to a plate and continue cooking the remaining chicken.
8. Add pepper and salt.
9. Put off the pot or keep it in warm.
10. Pour chicken broth over it and stir gently.
11. Now transfer the chicken into the Instant Pot and add half of the tomato mixture.
12. Close the lid and seal the vent.
13. Keep the cooking option to manual, and select high pressure and set timer for 7 minutes.
14. When the cooking over, allow it to settle the pressure for five minutes. After that release the pressure by using quick release.
15. Remove the chicken to a serving bowl.
16. Pour the remaining tomato sauce over it.
17. Garnish it with chopped fresh basil.
18. Serve hot

Nutritional values: Calories: 218 | Fats: 6g | Proteins: 32g | Carbohydrates: 5g | Cholesterol: 96mg | Sodium: 256mg | Potassium: 723mg | Sugar: 3g | Fiber: 0g

LOW CARB BELIZEAN STEWED CHICKEN

Preparation Time: 10 minutes | Cooking: 25 minutes | Serves: 8

Ingredients:

- Chicken legs - 4
- Coconut oil – 1 tablespoon
- Recado Rojo or any seasoning paste – 2 tablespoons
- White vinegar – 2 tablespoon
- Worcestershire sauce – 3 tablespoon
- Yellow onions, sliced – 1 cup
- Garlic clove, sliced - 3
- Grounded cumin – 1 teaspoon
- Dried oregano – 1 teaspoon
- Black pepper, grounded - ½ teaspoon
- Granulated sugar substitute – 1 tablespoon
- Chicken stock – 2 cups
- DON'T ADD SALT

Instructions:

1. In a large bowl, combine all the Recado or seasoning paste with Worcestershire sauce, oregano, pepper, cumin, sweetener, and vinegar.
2. Mix well.
3. Add all the chicken pieces and then rub the marinade inside the skin. Marinate it for at least one hour or overnight.
4. Place the insert inside the Instant Pot and then set it to sauté.
5. Heat the coconut oil and then brown the chicken in batches, skin sides down for approx. 2 minutes per side (keep the remaining marinade for late use)
6. Remove all the seared chicken on a plate and then set it aside.
7. Add all the onions and the garlic to the Instant Pot and then sauté it for 2-3 minutes until it becomes soft.
8. Put all the chicken pieces into the Instant Pot.
9. Now pour the remaining marinade and chicken broth over the chicken and stir.
10. Cover the Instant Pot and vent.
11. Set the Instant Pot manual High pressure for 20 minutes.
12. When timer goes off, release the pressure manually.
13. Before serving, check the sauce for taste and add salt as required.
14. Garnish with cilantro.
15. Serve hot.

Nutritional values: Calories: 319 | Fats: 22g | Proteins: 28g | Carbohydrates: 3g

SHREDDED CHICKEN TACO MEAT

Preparation Time: 5 minutes | Cooking: 50 minutes | Serves: 4

Ingredients:

- Chicken breasts - 4
- Bell peppers, sliced - 4
- Onion, sliced - 1
- Paprika – 2 tablespoons
- Garlic powder – 2 tablespoons
- Cumin powder – 1 tablespoon
- Chili powder – 1 teaspoon
- Ghee or coconut oil – 3 tablespoons
- Salt – to taste
- Black pepper - ½ teaspoon

Instructions:

1. Put all of the ingredients such as chicken, seasoning, oil, bell peppers, and onion into an Instant Pot and mix all the ingredients.

2. Close the lid and vent.

3. Set the Instant Pot to manual high pressure for 25 minutes.

4. Let the pressure release by itself.

5. Transfer the chicken to a bowl and shred the chicken meat.

6. Put back the shredded chicken along with seasoning and cook for about 2-3 minutes in sauté mode.

7. Add extra seasoning for taste, if required

8. Garnish with lettuce or kale leaves along with guacamole.

9. Serve hot.

Nutritional values: Calories: 230 | Fats: 12g | Proteins: 19g | Carbohydrates: 12g

BEEF AND PORK

BEEF BARBACOA

Preparation: 30 minutes | Cooking: 1 hour and 20 minutes | Serves: 9

Ingredients:

- Garlic – 5 cloves
- Onion, medium – ½
- Lime juice – 1
- Chipotles in adobo sauce – 2-4 teaspoons
- Cumin, ground) – 1 teaspoon
- Oregano, ground – 1 teaspoon
- Ground cloves – ½ teaspoon
- Water – 1 cup

- Beef eye of round/bottom round roast – 3 pounds
- Kosher salt – 2 & ½ teaspoons
- Black pepper – 2 teaspoons
- Oil – 1 teaspoon
- Bay leaf - 3

Cooking directions:

1. Mix garlic, onion, lime juice, oregano, cumin, cloves, chipotles, and water into a fine puree paste by using a blender.
2. Completely remove the fat from the meat and cut it into 3-inch pieces.
3. Season the meat with pepper and salt.
4. Set the Instant Pot on Sauté mode high.
5. Once the cooker turns hot enough, add oil and brown the meat pieces entirely in batches for about 5 minutes.
6. Add the pureed paste from the blender in the pot, add bay leaves and stir the meat occasionally.
7. Close the lid and vent of the Instant Pot.
8. Set the manual high pressure cook for one hour.
9. After cooking, allow it to release the pressure naturally.
10. When the complete pressure released, open the lid and check the tenderness of the meat using a fork. It must be cooked well within an hour.
11. Once the meat is tender enough, take out and discard the bay leaf and discard the water completely (reserve the liquid for later use).
12. Shred the meat by using two forks.
13. Now, add the salt, ½ teaspoon cumin, pepper and pour 1½ cup of reserved liquid and heat again for 2-3 minutes.
14. Your dish is ready, and you can serve it warm.

Nutritional values: Calories: 153 | Total Fats: 4.6g | Net Carbs: 2g | Protein: 24g | Fiber: 800mg | Cholesterol: 44mg |Sodium: 334mg | Potassium: 0mg | Sugar: 0g

INSTANT POT BALSAMIC ROAST BEEF

Preparation: 5 minutes | Cooking: 50 minutes | Serves: 8

Function: Slow Cook – Instant Pot

Ingredients:

- Boneless chuck roast (approximately 3 pounds) – 1
- Kosher salt - tablespoon
- Black ground pepper - 1 tablespoon
- Garlic powder - 1 tablespoon
- Balsamic vinegar - ¼ cup
- Water - 2 cup
- Onion, (chopped) - ½ cup
- Salt to taste
- Xanthan gum - ¼ tablespoon
- Fresh parsley, chopped - as required

Cooking directions:

1. Cut chuck roast into two pieces and put it in a bowl.
2. Add salt, garlic powder, and pepper into it and season it properly.
3. Set the instant pot to 'sauté' mode and put the roast pieces.
4. Sauté it until both sides become brown for about 6 minutes.
5. Now add ½ cup onion, ¼ cup balsamic vinegar and 1 cup water to the meet.
6. Cover the instant cooker and seal.
7. Set the timer manual high pressure for 35 minutes.
8. Release the pressure manually when the timer finishes.
9. Open the pot after releasing the full pressure.
10. Take out the meat carefully from the pan to a big bowl.
11. Break them into chunks and eliminate all large fatty pieces.
12. With the use of sautéing feature of your pot bring the liquid to a boil in the pan, and cook it for about 10 minutes to condense.
13. Now whip in the xanthan gum, and add the meat back to the pan to mix gently.
14. Turn off the pan temperature.
15. Serve hot garnishing with fresh chopped parsley.

Nutritional values: Calories: 393 | Total Fats: 28g | Net Carbs: 3g | Protein: 30g | Cholesterol: 113mg | Sodium: 173mg | Sugars: 1.4g

INSTANT POT BUTTER BEEF

Preparation Time: 10 minutes | Cooking: 1 hour 10 minutes | Serves: 6

Ingredients:

- Roast beef, chuck or arm – 3 pounds
- Olive oil – 1 tablespoon
- Ranch dressing seasoning mix – 2 tablespoons
- One jar pepper rings, drained with ¼ cup of juice reserved
- Zesty Italian seasoning mix – 2 tablespoons
- Butter – 8 tablespoons
- Water – 1 cup

Instructions:

1. Turn the Instant Pot to sauté or brown. Put in a tablespoon of olive oil into the bottom of the pot while it is hot.

2. Put the beef into the pot and sear both sides of the roast. It will take about 8 minutes.

3. Turn off the pot and then pour in the water along with seasoning mixes, and pepper rings, as well as the reserved juices on the top of roast beef.

4. Then place the butter on the top of the roast.

5. Lock the lid of the Instant Pot and then seal the pressure valve.

6. Set the Instant Pot manual high pressure cook for 60 minutes.

7. After the cooking is over, you could either allow for the natural release or go for the quick release.

8. Open the lid after a while and cut the beef using a salad sheer or break them apart using forks.

9. Serve it with pureed cauliflower or along with mashed potatoes.

Nutritional values: Calories: 857.7 | Carbs: 6.2g | Protein: 31.4g | Fat: 78g

INSTANT POT KETO MEAT BALLS

Preparation: 10 minutes | Cooking: 20 minutes | Serves: 5

Ingredients:

- Ground Beef – 1½ pounds
- Parsley, fresh chopped – 2 teaspoons
- Parmesan cheese, grated – 2 teaspoons
- Almond flour – ½ cup
- Egg – 2
- Kosher Salt – 1 teaspoon
- Black Pepper ground – ¼ teaspoon
- Garlic Powder – ¼ teaspoon
- Onion flakes dry – 1 teaspoon
- Oregano dry – ¼ teaspoon
- Water warm – ⅓ cup
- Olive oil – 1 teaspoon
- Marinara sauce as per requirement.

Cooking directions:

1. Take a medium bowl and combine the meatball ingredient and mix the meat using your hand.

2. Make an approximate 12-inch meatball from the ground beef.

3. Take an Instant Pot and spread some olive oil at the bottom.

4. In case if you want brown meatballs, then switch to the 'sauté' function of the pot and brown each side of the meatballs as needed. Or you can also cook them until brown in ordinary pan.

5. Don't press down the meatballs; place them in the pot at a distance without touching each other to avoid them from sticking.

6. Pour the marinara sauce as per your taste bud over the meatballs and seal the pot according to the instructions of the pan.

7. Now, set the pot to 'Manual' low pressure cook for 10 minutes.

8. Once the timer for 10 minutes goes off, turn the valve around to let the steam dissipate entirely.

9. Remove the lid and serve the meatballs hot with spaghetti, pasta or any particular side as needed.

Nutritional values: Calories: 455 | Total Fats: 33g | Net Carbs: 5g | Protein: 34g | Fiber: 1g | Cholesterol: 74mg | Sodium: 27mg | Potassium: 0mg | Sugars: 0mg

INSTANT POT NO-NOODLE LASAGNA

Preparation Time: 10 minutes | Cooking: 25 minutes | Serves: 8

Ingredients:

- Ground beef – 1 pound
- Onion – 1 small
- Garlic minced – 2 cloves
- Parmesan cheese - ½ cup
- Ricotta cheese - 1½ cup
- Marinara sauce – 1 Jar (25 ounces)
- Egg – 1 large
- Mozzarella sliced – 8 ounces

Instructions:

1. Set your Instant Pot to sauté and brown the ground beef with the onion and garlic for 10 minutes.
2. While the meat is cooking, combine Parmesan, ricotta cheese and egg in a mixing bowl.
3. Remove the grease and the browned beef to a 1½ quart dish that can fit into the Instant Pot.
4. Add marinara sauce to the browned meat.
5. Keep aside half of the meat sauce.
6. Top the rest of the meat sauce with the half of the mozzarella cheese.
7. Spread half of the ricotta cheese mixture on top of the mozzarella layer and the remaining with meat sauce.
8. Spread a layer of mozzarella above the meat.
9. Keep some mozzarella to spread on the last layer.
10. Spread the rest of the ricotta cheese on top of mozzarella.
11. Use the remaining mozzarella for final topping.
12. Cover the lasagne with an aluminum foil to prevent condensation from falling on the cheese. It is not needed if you want to reserve the top layer of cheese to add after the pressure cooking is over.
13. Place a trivet in the instant pot and pour one cup of water into the instant pot.
14. Keep the dish on the trivet.
15. Use a hook to remove the dish easily when the cooking is over.
16. Cover and cook at high pressure for 8-10 minutes.
17. Release the pressure manually and remove the lid.
18. Add the reserved cheese on top.
19. Cover and let the cheese melt if needed.
20. Serve hot.

Nutritional values: Calories: 365 | Fats: 25g | Proteins: 25g | Carbohydrates: 4g

KETO GROUND BEEF AND BROCCOLI

Preparation: 5 minutes | Cooking: 15 minutes | Serves: 4

Ingredients:

- Ground beef - 1 pound
- Butter - 3 ounces
- Broccoli, finely chopped – 9 ounces
- Mayonnaise - ½ cup
- Salt to taste

Cooking Directions:

1. Wash the broccoli and chop it into small pieces.

2. You can use the stem too, just peel and dice into small pieces.

3. Set your Instant Pot to sauté mode.

4. Add some butter and cook the broccoli until it become soft.

5. Remove broccoli and set aside.

6. Add some butter enough to cook the beef and brown the beef.

7. Stop sautéing and change the cooking mode to high pressure for 12 minutes.

8. When the time elapse, do a quick pressure release manually.

9. Open the lid carefully and season it with salt and pepper as required.

10. Now set the cooker to sauté mode again add the cooked broccoli.

11. Stir the beef occasionally and continue cooking until the sauce start to boil.

12. Serve hot.

13. Top with butter/mayonnaise before serving.

Nutritional values: Calories: 648 | Protein: 33g | Fat: 54g | Carbohydrates: 5g

LOW CARB KETO CHILI BEEF

Preparation Time: 15 minutes | Cooking: 55 minutes | Serving: 10 cups

Ingredients:

- Ground beef - 2½ pounds
- Garlic, minced – 8 cloves
- Onion, chopped - ½ large
- Tomato paste – 6 ounces
- Diced tomatoes with liquid – 2 can (15 ounces each)
- Worcestershire sauce – 2 tablespoon
- Green chilies with liquid – 4 ounces
- Cumin – 2 tablespoons
- Chili powder - ½ tablespoon
- Salt – 1 teaspoon
- Black pepper powder – ½ teaspoon
- Dried oregano – 1 tablespoon
- Bay leaf (optional) – 1 medium

Instructions:

1. Select the "Sauté" setting on the Instant Pot.
2. Add the chopped onion and sauté for about 6-7 minutes, until it becomes translucent.
3. Increase the time to about 20 minutes, if you like caramelized onions.
4. Now, after adding the garlic, cook it about less than a minute.
5. Now put all the ground beef and cook for 8-10 minutes, breaking them apart with a spatula, until it becomes brown.
6. Excluding the bay leaf, add all the remaining ingredients to the Instant Pot and stir until combined.
7. Pour a cup of broth or water.
8. Place the bay leaf in the middle, if you are using it.
9. Stop the sautéing process and turn the cooker to 'meat or stew' setting. The default setting is 35 minutes or keeps the setting for 35 minutes.
10. Start the cooking option.
11. When the cooking over, allow it to release the pressure naturally.
12. Allow it to settle for some time before opening the lid.
13. Discard the bay leaf before serving.
14. Serve hot.

Nutritional Values: Calories: 306 | Fats: 18g | Proteins: 23g | Carbohydrates: 10g

INSTANT POT BEEF STROGANOFF

Preparation Time: 10 minutes | Cooking: 30 minutes | Servings: 4

Ingredients:

- Stewing Beef steak cubed – 1.1lb
- Mushroom quartered – 0.55lb
- Beef stock – 0.55lb
- Onion, sliced - 1
- Steaky bacon – 2 slices
- Garlic cloves – 2
- Paprika, smoked – 1 teaspoon
- Tomato paste – 3 tablespoon
- Sour cream (for garnishing)

Instructions:

1. Keep your instant pot and set to sauté mode.

2. When the pan becomes hot, pour some oil and sauté onion, bacon, and garlic.

3. Do not brown it, but let it become translucent.

4. Add the cubed beef and sauté it until it becomes brown on all sides.

5. Add tomato paste, paprika, mushrooms and sauté.

6. Now pour beef broth and stir.

7. Close the lid and seal the vent.

8. Keep the cooking option to manual, and select high pressure and set timer for 30 minutes.

9. When the cooking over, allow it to settle the pressure for five minutes. After that release the pressure by using quick release.

10. Remove the chicken to a serving bowl.

11. Garnish it with sour cream.

12. Serve hot.

Nutritional values: Calories: 317 | Fats: 19g | Proteins: 29g | Carbohydrates: 8g | Fiber: 1g | Sugars: 4g

MISSISSIPPI ROAST BEEF

Preparation: 10 minutes | Cooking: 1 hour | Serves: 8

Ingredients:

- Boneless beef chuck roast – 3 to 4 pounds
- Butter – 8 tablespoons
- Beef broth - ½ cup
- Onion, finely chopped - ½ onion
- Dry Ranch dressing mix – 1 package
- Pepperoncini peppers – to taste
- Freshly ground peppers – as needed
- Salt to taste
- Mayonnaise – 2 tablespoons
- Apple cider vinegar – 2 tablespoons

Cooking directions:

1. In the insert port of your Instant Pot, combine Ranch seasoning, beef broth, and chopped onion. Continue mixing until it mixes thoroughly.
2. Season beef chuck roast with salt, pepper, butter and pepperoncini in a bowl and add to the insert pot.
3. Close the lid and set to pressure cook for one hour.
4. As this process goes on, make a ranch dressing.
5. Combine the mayonnaise, vinegar in a small bowl.
6. After completing the cooking let it release the pressure naturally for 15 minutes.
7. Open the lid and transfer the meat to a large bowl.
8. Shred the meat by using two forks.
9. Toss the meat with the remaining gravy of the cooker.
10. Serve hot with the dressing.

Nutritional values: Calories: 377 | Total Carbohydrate: 1.6g | Protein: 30g | Sodium: 509.5mg | Total Fat: 26.8g | Potassium: 399mg | Fiber: 0g

CREAMY PARMESAN GARLIC PORK CHOPS

Preparation: 5 minutes | Cooking: 20 minutes | Serves: 6

Ingredients:

- Boneless pork chops 4-5 (app.3-4 ounces)
- Salt and pepper to taste
- Salted butter - 1½
- Garlic cloves, minced - 3
- Heavy cream - 1½ cup
- All-purpose flour - 2 tablespoons.
- Parmesan, grated - ¾ cup
- Fresh parsley, minced - 1 tablespoon

Cooking directions:

1. Select Sauté mode in the Instant Pot, add butter and allow to melt until it spread in the pan.

2. Season the pork meat pieces with salt and pepper on both sides.

3. Place pork in the pot and cook on both sides about 4-5 minutes until it becomes golden brown.

4. Stop sautéing.

5. Transfer it to a tight lid container and keep it there for 10 minutes

6. Now sauté garlic in the pot and allow to caramelize or 2 minutes until the raw smell goes off.

7. Stop sautéing and add the flour and cream.

8. Stir continuously to combine.

9. Now close the lid and set it manual high pressure cook for 2 minutes.

10. Once the cooking over, release the pressure manually.

11. Open the lid and stir in the grated parmesan and fresh parsley.

12. Stir the food.

13. Serve with sauce.

Nutritional values: Calories: 529 | Fat: 36.5g | Protein: 48.9g | Carbs: 2.7g | Fiber: 200mg

INSTANT POT PORK RIBS

Preparation time: 15 minutes | Cooking: 45 minutes | Serves: 6

Function: Slow Cook

Ingredients:

- Pork ribs cut pieces – 5 pounds

For dry seasoning:

- Erythritol or any sweetener – 1 tablespoon
- Ground black pepper – ½ tablespoon
- Garlic powder – 1 teaspoon
- Onion powder – 1 teaspoon
- Paprika – 1 teaspoon
- Allspice – ½ teaspoon
- Ground coriander – ½ teaspoon
- Kosher salt – 1.5 tablespoon

For the sauce:

- Reduced sugar ketchup – ½ cup
- Erythritol or other sweetener – 2 tablespoons
- Red wine vinegar – 2 tablespoons
- Water – ½ cup
- Liquid smoke – ¼ teaspoon
- Ground mustard – ½ tablespoon
- Ground allspice – ½ tablespoon
- Onion powder – ½ teaspoon
- Xanthan gum – ¼ teaspoon (Optional)

Cooking directions:

1. Rub the dry seasoning ingredients on all the sides of the ribs.
2. Now, take the ribs and place it in the Instant Pot.
3. Take a small bowl and add the ketchup, sweetener, water, liquid smoke, vinegar, mustard, allspice, onion powder and stir well.
4. Pour the mix over the ribs.
5. Close the Instant Pot lid and set the timer for thirty-five minutes on manual high pressure cook.

6. After cooking, release the pressure and remove the lid.
7. Now, take a platter and place the ribs over it and keep it warm.
8. Into the sauce, put the xanthan gum and whisk well.
9. Now, turn the sauté function key on and cook the leftover liquid for about ten minutes.
10. Pour the sauce on the cooked pork and serve hot.

Nutritional values: Calories: 1,691 | Total Fat: 134.1g |Carbohydrates: 2.1g | Dietary Fiber: 4g | Sugars: 1.6g | Protein: 110.6g | Cholesterol: 534.9mg | Sodium: 1,116.6mg | Potassium: 1,508mg

INSTANT POT BONELESS PORK CHOPS

Preparation: 5 minutes | Cooking: 5 minutes | Serves: 5

Ingredients:

- Coconut oil – 1 tablespoon
- Ranch mix – 1 package
- Butter(or margarine) – ½ cup
- Boneless pork chops – 6
- Water – 1 cup

Cooking directions:

1. Place the pork chops in the Instant Pot.

2. Add a tablespoon full of coconut oil in it.

3. Select the sauté mode and start browning both of its sides. Make sure that the pork chops get browned from all the sides. You can even omit this step. But, the pork chops look more delicious when cooked to brown.

4. Spread the ranch mix packet after putting the butter on the top.

5. Now, pour a glass of water over it. You can even use chicken broth for that purpose.

6. Now, close your instant pot and its vent.

7. Set the Instant Pot to manual high pressure for five minutes.

8. Let the pressure release naturally for the next five minutes and then, quickly release the remaining pressure manually.

9. Serve hot.

10. Also, you can even garnish the butter sauce over your dish to make it look even more delicious.

Nutritional values: Calories: 299.1 | Fat: 147g | Carbohydrates: 6.9g | Cholesterol: 89.5mg | Sodium: 750.2mg | Potassium: 457.5mg | Protein: 32.7g | Sugars: 1g

INSTANT POT CREAMY GARLIC PORK CHOPS

Preparation time: 10 minutes | Cooking: 15 minutes |Serves: 4

Ingredients:

- Progresso™ chicken broth – 1 cup
- Garlic cloves, finely chopped – 4
- Salt – 1 teaspoon
- Pepper – ½ teaspoon
- Pork loin chops with born – 1¾ pounds
- Cornstarch – 2 tablespoon
- Water – 2 tablespoon
- Cream cheese, cubed and softened – 4 ounces

Cooking directions:

1. Spray the instant pot with cooking spray and add broth to it.
2. Add garlic, pepper, and salt and stir to mix all.
3. Add pork chops to the pot and close the lid.
4. Choose 'manual' high pressure for 2 minutes.
5. Release the pressure quickly.
6. After cooking, remove pork chops from the pot and cover with foil paper to keep it warm.
7. Beat cornstarch and water together and choose sauté mode in low medium heat.
8. Whisk the solution frequently until thickened and stop sautéing.
9. Add cream cheese and whisk until completely smooth.
10. Pour the mixture over pork chops and serve hot.

Nutritional values: Calories: 340 | Total Fat: 21g | Carbohydrates: 7g | Dietary Fiber: 0g | Sugars: 1g | Protein: 33g | Cholesterol: 120mg | Sodium: 640mg | Potassium: 440mg

INSTANT POT LOW CARB PORK SAAG

Preparation time: 5 minutes | Cooking: 15 minutes | Serves: 6

Ingredients:

For marinade:

- Pork shoulder, cut into small pieces – 1 pound
- Half and a half – ⅓ cup
- Garlic, minced – 1 teaspoon
- Ginger, minced - 1 teaspoon
- Turmeric – ½ teaspoon
- Cayenne pepper - ½ teaspoon
- Salt - ½ teaspoon
- Garam Masala - 2 teaspoons

Other Ingredients:

- Oil or Ghee – 1 tablespoon
- Tomato paste – 1 tablespoon

- Water – ¾ cup
- Baby spinach – 5 ounces

Cooking directions:

1. Marinate the pork.
2. Set your Instant Pot to Sauté mode.
3. Pour cooking oil into the pot.
4. Once the oil is hot, add marinated pork pieces along with tomato paste. Mix the tomato paste and pork well and cook for 10 minutes until well mixed.
5. Stop sautéing.
6. Close the lid and pressure vent.
7. Set the pressure cooking manual high pressure for 10 minutes.
8. After cooking release the pressure manually.
9. Open the lid and add baby spinach and mix well.
10. Close the lid and pressure vent.
11. Set pressure cooking to manual high-pressure cook for 5 more minutes and let the pressure release on its own.
12. Mix well and garnish with half and a half.
13. Serve hot

Nutritional values: Calories: 120 | Total Fat: 7g | Carbohydrates: 2g | Dietary Fiber: 1g | Protein: 10g | Cholesterol: 42mg | Sodium: 469mg | Potassium: 333mg

INSTANT POT MEXICAN PORK CARNITAS

Preparation: 15 minutes | Cooking: 1 hour 25 minutes | Serves: 11

Ingredients:

- Trimmed, boneless pork shoulder blade roast – 2½ pounds
- Garlic – 6 cloves
- Black pepper to taste
- Cumin – 1½ teaspoons
- Sazon – ½ teaspoon
- Dry oregano – ¼ teaspoon
- Reduced sodium chicken broth – 1 cup
- Kosher salt – 2 teaspoons
- Chipotle peppers in adobo sauce to taste – 3
- Bay leaves – 2
- Dry adobo seasoning – ¼ teaspoon
- Garlic powder – ½ teaspoon

Cooking directions:

1. Add salt and pepper to pork and season it.
2. Turn on the sauté function of the Instant Pot and sprinkle some oil and start browning the pork on all of its sides for about five minutes.
3. Now, take the pork out and let it cool.
4. After that, with a sharp knife, make a cut about 1-inch deep in the pork.
5. Cut the garlic into slivers and insert it inside the cut.
6. Repeat the above step all over the pork.
7. Add cumin, oregano, sazon, and adobo and garlic powder over the pork.
8. Pour chicken broth over it.
9. Put some chipotle peppers and blend it.
10. Now, add bay leaves into it.
11. Put the pork inside the instant pot and seal the lid.
12. Select high-pressure mode and cook it for eighty minutes.
13. After releasing the pressure, take out the pork and shred it with the help of two forks.
14. Mix it well with the juices at the bottom of the pot.
15. Discard bay leaves and adjust the cumin and adobo as per your taste and mix it well.
16. Serve hot.

Nutritional values: Calories: 160 | Total Fat: 7g | Carbohydrates: 1g | Fiber: 0g | Cholesterol: 69 mg | Sodium: 397mg | Sugar: 0g | Protein: 20g

INSTANT POT SMOTHERED PORK CHOPS

Preparation Time: 10 minutes | Cooking: 35 minutes | Serves: 4

Ingredients:

- Pork chops, boneless loin cut – 6 ounces
- Garlic powder - 1 teaspoon
- Paprika – 1 tablespoon
- Onion powder - 1 teaspoon
- Black pepper - 1 teaspoon
- Salt - 1 teaspoon
- Cayenne pepper – ¼ teaspoon
- Coconut oil – 2 tablespoons
- Onion, sliced – ½ medium
- Baby Bella mushrooms, sliced – 6 ounces
- Butter - 1 tablespoon
- Heavy whipping cream – ½ cup
- Xanthan gum – ½ teaspoon
- Fresh parsley, chopped – 1 tablespoon

Cooking directions:

1. In a small bowl, mix paprika, onion powder, garlic powder, pepper, and salt.
2. Clean the pork and rub 1tbspn of spice mixture on both sides
3. On your Instant Pot, select sauté mode.
4. Add in coconut oil when the insert pot becomes hot and cook pork chops on both sides for 3 minutes until browned.
5. Turn off the pot and transfer the pork chops onto a serving plate.
6. Add sliced onions and mushrooms to the Instant Pot.
7. Place cooked pork on top of it.
8. Close the lid and set manual pressure cook for 25 minutes.
9. Once cooked, release the pressure either manually or naturally and transfer pork chops alone to a plate.
10. Put the pot in sauté setting and add remaining spice mix, heavy cream, and butter to the onion-mushroom mix.
11. Now add xanthan gum into the gravy mix and whisk properly.
12. Allow the gravy to simmer for about 5 minutes till the sauce start getting thick. Adjust the gravy to desired consistency. Keep in mind that the gravy will thicken once cooled.
13. Add the gravy to the top of pork chops.
14. Garnish with fresh parsley and enjoy it hot.

Nutritional values: Calories: 481.25 | Fat: 32.61g | Carbohydrates: 4.06g | Protein: 39.59g | Fiber: 2.42g

JAMAICAN JERK PORK ROAST

Preparation Time: 15 minutes | Cooking: 55 minutes | Serves: 12

Ingredients:

- Pork shoulder – 4 pounds
- Jamaican Jerk spice blend without sugar - ¼ cup
- Olive oil – 1 tablespoon
- Beef stock or broth - ½ cup

Instructions:

1. Polish the preparation with olive oil and coat with Jamaican Jerk zest mix.

2. Set your Instant Pot to Sauté and cook the meat until it becomes all side.

3. Add the beef broth.

4. Close the Instant Pot and set manual high pressure cook for 45 minutes.

5. Release pressure manually and allow it to settle for a while.

6. Serve hot.

Nutritional values: Calories: 282 | Fats: 20g | Proteins: 23g | Carbohydrates: 0g

PORK TENDERLOIN WITH CURRY SAUCE

Preparation Time: 20 minutes | Cooking: 45 minutes | Serve: 8

Ingredients:

- Pork Tenderloin – 1½ pounds
- Shredded leak – 1
- Butter – 4 ounces
- Green cabbage – 25 ounces
- Garam masala powder – 1 tablespoon
- Massive whipping bream – 1¼ cups
- Salt and pepper to taste

Cooking directions:

1. Chop the cabbage finely.
2. Select sauté mode in the Instant Pot.
3. Add 1 teaspoon butter and sauté the Cabbage soft.
4. Stir occasionally and season with salt and pepper and keep it aside.
5. Slice the tenderloin into fine pieces and cook with remaining butter in sauté mode.
6. Sear until it becomes brown.
7. Stop sautéing.
8. Wash the finely shredded leek and put over it.
9. Add cream, garam masala powder.
10. Close the Instant Pot and set to manual high pressure cook for 35 minutes.
11. Let it release the pressure naturally.
12. After cooking open the lid.
13. Season with salt and pepper to taste.
14. Serve with butter fried cabbage.

Nutritional values: Calories: 712 | Fat: 56g | Carbohydrates: 9g | Protein: 40g | Fiber: 6g

PORK AND TOMATILLO CHILI

Preparation: 15 minutes | Cooking: 50 minutes | Serves: 8

Ingredients:

- Ground pork – 2 pound
- Tomatillos chopped – 3
- White onion chopped – ½
- Tomato paste – 6 ounces
- Garlic powder – 1 teaspoon
- Jalapeno well chopped – 1
- Cumin ground – 1 teaspoon
- Chili powder – 1 teaspoon
- Salt – 1 teaspoon /as per taste.

Cooking directions:

1. In an Instant Pot, in sauté mode cook the pork until it turns brown.

2. Add the ingredients such as tomatillo, onion, tomato paste, jalapeno, garlic, cumin and chili powder as per the given measurement. Finally, add water and all the ingredients together thoroughly.

3. Press start/stop to stop the sauté mode.

4. Set the Instant Pot to pressure cooker mode and secure the lid and cook at high pressure for around 35 minutes and release the pressure manually once cooking is over.

5. You can serve the dish now with any low-carb topping as per your taste or add vegetables If required, it'll enhance the flavor and give additional siders to the plate.

Nutritional values: Calories: 325 | Total Fats: 23g | Net Carbs: 6g | Protein: 20g | Fiber: 1g | Cholesterol: 81mg | Sodium: 256mg | Potassium: 618mg | Sugars: 3g

PRESSURE COOKER PORK AND KRAUT

Preparation: 15 minutes | Cooking: 55 minutes | Serves: 4-6

Ingredients:

- Pork Roast – 3 pounds
- Organic coconut oil – 2 tablespoons (Or ghee, butter, lard, etc)
- Large onions, chopped – 2
- Garlic cloves, peeled and sliced – 3
- Filtered water – 1 cup
- Sea salt – to taste
- Freshly ground black pepper
- Sauerkraut – 4-6 cups
- Hot dogs (optional) – 1 pound
- Kielbasa (optional) – ½ pound

Cooking directions:

1. Liberally add sea salt to taste and pepper to your pork roast.
2. In the Instant Pot, select Sauté mode high heat.
3. When the pot becomes hot pour some coconut oil and start roasting pork until it becomes brown on both sides. Make sure to brown its edges as well.
4. Stop sautéing and add water, onions, and garlic.
5. Add sea salt and pepper as required.
6. Close the lid and vent.
7. Press the stew/meat button and set it to high pressure (Or standard pressure) and cook it for thirty-five minutes.
8. Allow to release the pressure naturally.
9. After releasing the pressure, add half of the sauerkraut into it. Add only half of it and balance you can serve raw to get the benefits of the fermented bacteria.
10. Cook the pork roast and sauerkraut under pressure for about five minutes if the pork is tender and if the pork is rough, cook it for about fifteen minutes.
11. Turn the release valve and release the pressure manually from the cooker.
12. Place hot dogs and kielbasa inside the pressure cooker and pressure cook for about five minutes.
13. Now, again, turn the release valve manually and release the pressure from the cooker.
14. Let it cool and add some mashed potatoes to your dish.
15. Serve the dish with krauts of both - raw and cooked.

Nutritional values: Calories: 387 | Total Fat: 32g | Cholesterol: 86mg | Carbohydrates: 8g | Protein: 18g | Sodium: 601mg | Potassium: 431mg | Sugars: 0g

SMOTHERED PORK CHOPS WITH BACON AND CARAMELIZED ONION

Preparation time: 10 minutes | Cooking: 60 minutes | Serves: 4

Ingredients:

- Finely chopped bacon – 6 slices
- Thinly sliced small onions - 2
- Salt – ¼ teaspoon
- Pepper - ¼ teaspoon
- Bones in pork chops (1 inch thick) – 4
- Chicken broth – ½ cup
- Heavy cream – ¼ cup
- Salt & pepper to taste

Cooking directions:

1. In your Instant Pot, sauté bacon over medium heat until crispy.

2. Add onions to bacon and sprinkle with salt and pepper.

3. Stir continuously for 15 to 20 minutes until it becomes transparent and Golden brown.

4. Add pork chops to pot and bring it to brown color on either side.

5. Stop sautéing.

6. Change the cooking mode to manual high pressure for 35 minutes.

7. When cooking over allow it to release the pressure naturally.

8. Transfer the food to a foil coated plate.

9. Add broth to the pot and add cream and select sauté mode.

10. Continue sautéing until it becomes thick for 2 to 3 minutes

11. Add onions and bacon to pan and stir for a right combination.

12. Garnish pork chops with onion and bacon mixture and serve hot.

Nutritional values: Calories: 352 | Protein: 36.98g | Sodium: 725mg | Cholesterol: 107mg | Net Carbohydrates: 5.28g | Total Fat: 18.23g | Saturated Fatty Acids: 8.43g

DESSERTS

LOW-CARB CREAMY RICE PUDDING

Preparation time: 10 minutes | Cooking: 10 minutes | Serves: 6

Ingredients:

- Low carb sweetener - ¼ cup
- Eggs - 3
- Miracle rice – 7 ounces
- Vanilla extract - 1 teaspoon
- Coconut cream/coconut milk – 13.5 ounces
- Nutmeg - ½ teaspoon

Method:

1. Using a large bowl, rinse the rice in water and drain it.

2. In your Instant Pot, saute the rice with no oil. Once the rice is dry, remove it and set aside.

3. In a mixing bowl, combine vanilla, eggs, sweetener, coconut cream and water by using a blender.

4. Put rice in the Instant Pot.

5. Add the cream mixture to the Instant Pot and combine.

6. Sprinkle nutmeg on top.

7. Close the lid, and set the Instant Pot to high-pressure cook for 3 minutes.

8. After elapsing the cooking time, let it release the pressure naturally for 10 minutes.

9. Release the remaining pressure manually.

10. Refrigerate the pudding for about 10 - 15 minutes.

11. A few raspberries can also add, which can give extra flavor and tangy punch to the pudding.

Nutritional values: Calories: 180 | Carbohydrates: 3.8g | Fat: 17.4g | Cholesterol: 82mg | Sodium: 40mg | Fiber: 1.4g | Protein: 4.2g | Sugars: 2.4g

INSTANT POT DULCE DE LECHE CHEESECAKE

Preparation Time: 10 minutes | Cooking: 35 minutes | Serves: 6

Ingredients:

For making the crust:

- Shortbread cookies – 1 cup
- Melted butter – 4 tablespoons

For Dulce de Leche Cheesecake:

- Dulce de Leche – 1 can (13.4 ounces)
- Eggs, kept in room temperature – 2 large

- Egg yolk, room temperature – 1
- Cream cheese, room temperature – 16 ounces
- Flour – 3 tablespoons

For topping:

- Dulce de Leche – 1 can (13.4 ounces)
- Salt – optional

Method:

Make the crust:

1. Use a 7-inch springform pan that can fit inside your Instant Pot.
2. Spray its inside with non-stick spray.
3. Place a parchment paper inside the pan.
4. In the food processor, ground the cookies.
5. Now mix the crumbled cookies with melted butter in a bowl.
6. Press the mixture to the bottom and side of the pan.
7. Keep it in the refrigerator and continue working on the filling.

Make the filling:

1. Beat the cream cheese for about 3-4 minutes in a mixer until it becomes smooth.
2. Add egg one by one and beat it thoroughly.
3. Scrape down the sides of the bowl.
4. Now add the flour and continue mixing.
5. Add full Dulce De Leche and mix thoroughly.
6. Transfer the entire mix over the crust prepared in the springform pan.
7. Cover it with aluminum foil.
8. For easy handling, you can make an aluminum sling by folding it into 3. It is okay if you can manage without using a sling.
9. Now pour 1½ cup of water into the Instant Pot and place a trivet on it.

10. Place the springform pan on it.

11. Clot the lid of the cook and shut the vent.

12. Set the cooker to manual high pressure for 35 minutes.

13. After 35 minutes, wait for 10 minutes before you can release the pressure manually.

14. Open the lid and take out the springform pan and remove the aluminum foil.

15. The center of the cake should be slightly jiggly.

16. Allow it cool for about 20-25 minutes.

Make the toppings:

1. Set your Instant Pot into Sauté mode and pour Dulce De Leche and bring to medium heat and continue stirring.

2. When it becomes soft and fluid condense stage, pour on top of the cheesecake.

3. Spread it with a cooking spoon or knife.

4. Refrigerate for about 6 hours or more.

5. You can also top it with salt sprinkles.

Nutritional values: Calories: 376 | Fat: 36g | Carbs: 7g | Cholesterol: 190mg | Sodium: 338mg | Potassium: 124mg | Protein: 7g | Sugars: 5g

INSTANT POT KETO LEMON RICOTTA CHEESECAKE

Preparation: 10 minutes | Cooking: 40 minutes | Serves: 6

Ingredients:

- Cream cheese – 8 ounces
- Truvia – ¼ cup
- Ricotta cheese – ⅓ cup
- Zest of one lemon
- Lemon juice from one lemon
- Lemon extract – ½ teaspoon
- Eggs – 2

For topping:

- Sour cream – 2 tablespoon
- Truvia – 1 teaspoon

Cooking directions:

1. Mix cream cheese, Truvia, ricotta cheese, lemon zest, lemon juice, lemon extract together with the help of a hand mixer. Continue mixing until it becomes smooth and free from the chunks.

2. Taste this mixture once to ensure that the sweetness is as per your taste or liking.

3. Now, add the eggs in the mixture and gently blend at a lesser speed. Mix it until the eggs get absorbed into the batter. Do not over-beat the mixture otherwise; it will lead to a cracker crust.

4. Take a 6-inch spring-form pan and add the mixture into it. Grease the pan before your transfer the dough into it.

5. Cover the pan with a foil. You can also use the silicone lid for this purpose.

6. Take two cups of water and put it inside the inner liner of the Instant Pot.

7. Now, place the trivet and put the pan over the trivet in the instant pot.

8. Set it on high pressure and cook for about thirty minutes.

9. Let the pressure of the instant pot release naturally.

10. Now, blend the sour cream and Truvia for the topping.

11. Spread the prepared topping on the warm cake.

12. Refrigerate the cake for about 6-8 hours.

13. Serve it cold.

Nutritional values: Calories: 181 | Total Fat: 16g | Saturated Fat: 9g | Cholesterol: 105mg | Sodium: 156mg | Potassium: 86mg | Total Carbohydrates: 2g | Sugars: 1g | Protein: 5g

INSTANT POT MATCHA CHEESECAKE

Preparation time: 5 minutes | Cooking: 5 minutes | Serves: 6

Ingredients:

For the cake:

- Cream cheese, room temperature – 16 ounces
- Swerve confectioners - ½ cup
- Coconut flour – 2 teaspoons
- Vanilla extract - ½ teaspoons
- Eggs – 2 large
- Matcha powder – 1 tablespoon
- Heavy whipping cream – 2 tablespoons
- Maple syrup, sugar free - optional

For topping:

- Sour cream - ½ cup
- Swerve confectioners – 2 teaspoons

Method:

1. Put vanilla extract, coconut flour, whipping cream, cream cheese, matcha powder and Swerve in a mixing bowl and combine well.

2. Add eggs one by one.

3. Take a spring form pan of 6-7-inches diameter that can fit inside your Instant Pot and transfer the batter into the pan.

4. Pour 1½ water into to the bottom of the Instant Pot and place the trivet or steam tray on it.

5. Close the lid and the vent.

6. Set the cooker to manual high pressure for 35 minutes.

7. After cooking let it release the pressure naturally for 20 minutes.

8. Open the lid. If you see any water drops on the cake absorb it with a paper towel.

9. Now prepare the topping.

10. Mix Serve confectioners and sour cream and spread on top of the cake.

11. Allow it to cool and then refrigerate it for 4-6 hours or more.

12. Sprinkle with matcha powder while serving.

13. Optionally, you can drizzle some sugar free maple syrup.

Nutritional values: Calories: 350.33 | Total Fats: 33.24g | Net Carbs: 5.81g | Protein: 8.46g

INSTANT POT PUMPKIN CHEESECAKE

Preparation: 20 minutes | Cooking: 50 minutes | Serves: 8

Ingredients:

Graham Cracker Crust:

- Graham crackers - 8
- Sugar – 2 teaspoons
- Melted butter - 2½ tablespoons
- Cinnamon - ¼ teaspoons
- Ginger powder - ¼ teaspoons

Cheesecake filling:

- Cream cheese, kept in room temperature – 16 ounces
- Pumpkin puree (Pure) – 1 cup
- Cinnamon - ¼ teaspoon
- Vanilla – 2 teaspoon
- Sugar - ½ cup

- Heavy cream, kept in room temperature - ½ cup
- Pumpkin Pie spice - ¾ teaspoon
- Nutmeg - ½ teaspoon
- All-purpose flour – 2 teaspoon
- Eggs – 3
- Allspice - ¾ teaspoon
- Ginger powder - ¼ teaspoon

Optional: To make it sweeter

- Brown sugar - ¼ cup

For Garnishing:

- Whipped cream + cinnamon powder

Cooking directions:

1. Use a 7 or 8-inch springform pan or cheesecake pan, which sit inside your Instant Pot.

2. Spray some non-stick baking spray in the pan.

3. Place a parchment paper in the bottom of the pan and spray the baking spray also over the parchment paper.

4. In your Instant Pot, pour 1½ cup water and place trivet on it.

5. Now take your food processor and place the crushed graham crackers.

6. Add ginger powder, sugar, and cinnamon.

7. Pulse all the items to become smooth crumbs.

8. Add melted butter and blend it to combine thoroughly.

9. Transfer the mix to the parchment paper laid pan and press it evenly by using a flat glass bottom.

10. Cover the entire bottom of the pan with a little side extension. No need to cover the whole sides.

11. Place the pan in the refrigerator and continue preparing cheesecake filling.

12. Clean the food processor and add sugar and cheese. If you want the cheesecake sweeter, add the optional brown sugar.

13. Pulse it, until it becomes smooth and soft creamy.

14. Now add pumpkin puree, vanilla, spices, heavy cream, and flour.

15. Pulse all the above until it becomes smooth cream.

16. Add eggs and spin it for a short period.

17. Take the processor bowl out and mix the egg by hand and mix it properly.

18. If you mix the egg with the processor, it may spoil the thickness and texture of the cake. So be careful while mixing the eggs.

19. Now take crust from the refrigerator and transfer the filling over it.

20. Cover the pan with a paper towel and also cover it by using aluminum foil.

21. Crimp the edges of the pan with the aluminum foil.

22. Place the pan on the trivet and close the lid.

23. Set your Instant Pot to manual high-pressure cook mode for 55 minutes.

24. After finish cooking, let the pressure release naturally for 20 minutes. After that release the remaining pressure manually. Let it cool for 10 more minutes.

25. Open the lid and take out the pan.

26. Check the center of the cake to find out whether it is too soft. If it is too soft, you can cook it further 10 more minutes.

27. After cooking over, let it cool for about 1 hour and refrigerate it for 4 hours or more.

28. Top it with whipped cream and sprinkle some cinnamon powder.

Nutritional values: Calories: 273 | Fat: 25g | Net Carbohydrates: 4.5g | Protein: 4g | Cholesterol: 28mg | Sodium: 114mg | Potassium: 77mg

KETO BUTTERCREAM

Preparation Time: 5 minutes | Cooking: 10 minutes | Serves: 4

Ingredients:

- Unsalted butter – 8¼ ounces
- Vanilla extract - 2 teaspoon
- Ground cinnamon - 1½ teaspoon
- Erythritol – 1 or 2 teaspoons (optional)

Method:

1. Set your Instant Pot to Sauté mode and melt ¼ of the butter until its color changes to amber. Be careful not to burn it.

2. Now pour the brown butter into a bowl and whisk the remaining butter by using a hand mixer until it turns fluffy

3. Serve by topping it with cinnamon and sweetener.

Nutritional values: Calories: 412 | Total Fats: 46g | Net Carbs: 1g | Protein: 1g | Fiber: 1g | Cholesterol: 10mg | Sodium: 225mg | Potassium: 201mg | Sugars: 5g

KETO DAIRY-FREE VANILLA CUSTARD

Preparation: 5 minutes | Cooking: 5 minutes | Serves: 4

Ingredients:

- Egg yolks - 6
- Unsweetened almond milk - ½ cup
- Vanilla extract - 1 teaspoon
- Erythritol (optional) - 1 teaspoon

Cooking directions:

1. Beat all the ingredients like egg yolks, vanilla, almond milk, (optional sweetener) in a medium-size bowl.

2. Pour the mix into a Pressure Cooker safe bowl.

3. Cover the bowl with an aluminum foil. Make some venting holes on the foil.

4. Pour 1½ cup water to the bottom of the Instant Pot.

5. Place a trivet in the Instant Pot and put the bowl on the trivet.

6. Close the lid and put the cooking setting to High Pressure for 7 minutes.

7. After cooking allow it to release the pressure naturally for 10 minutes and after that manually release the remaining pressure.

8. Serve it either hot or chilled.

Nutritional values: Calories: 215 | Total Fats: 21g | Net Carbs: 1g | Protein: 4g | Fiber: 0g

KETO PUMPKIN LAYER CHEESECAKE

Preparation: 15 minutes | Cooking: 55 minutes | Servings: 8 slices

Ingredients:

For Crust:

- Almond Flour – ½ cup
- Pecan Halves very finely chopped – ½ cup
- Cinnamon – 1 teaspoon
- Lakanto Powdered Monk fruit Sweetener – 1 tablespoon
- Grass-Fed Butter softened but not melted – 2 tablespoon

Cheesecake Layer:

- Cream Cheese room temperature – 8 ounces
- Lakanto Classic Monk fruit Sweetener – ¼ cup + 1 tablespoon
- Vanilla Extract – ¼ teaspoon

- Fresh Orange Zest – 1 teaspoon Or Orange Extract dried zest results in a chunky texture – ⅛ teaspoon
- Egg room temperature – 1
- Heavy whipping cream – 2 tablespoon

Pumpkin Layer:

- Pumpkin Puree – ¼ cup
- Pumpkin Pie Spice – ½ teaspoon

Serving:

- LCHF Whipped Cream
- Ground Cinnamon optional

Cooking Directions:

1. Take a bowl and add almond flour, cinnamon, finely chopped pecans, and monk fruit. Mix them well with a fork evenly and break the chunks apart, if any.

2. Now, add the softened butter in the mixture.

3. Cut it with the help of a fork until the mixture becomes friable, but also it can hold its shape.

4. Take a spring-form or push-pan and transfer the mixture into it. The pan should be 6" or 7" size, and the mixture should go about an inch above the sides.

5. Mix cream cheese, heavy cream, orange peel, vanilla, and monk fruit together with the help of a stand mixer or hand-held mixer. Blend it until it becomes smooth.

6. Add the egg in the mixture.

7. Mix it gently until it looks just and smooth. Do not mix it more than that is required. Over-mixing will make the cake lumpy.

8. Pour this mixture over the pan and keep one cup of batter aside.

9. Take pumpkin puree and pumpkin pie spice and add to batter kept aside. Blend it well but do not over-mix it.

10. Put this mixture in the pan over the cream cheese mixture carefully. Ensure that the dough is spread evenly along the edges as well.

11. Take a paper towel and place it on the top of the pan. Cover the top gently with a piece of tin foil and crimp the edges.

12. Now, take about 1½ cup of water and pour it in the inner liner pot of the Instant Pot.

13. Place the trivet on it and put the pan over it.

14. Close the Instant Pot and set the cooker to manual high pressure for thirty-seven minutes.

15. After cooking, for about eighteen minutes, allow the pressure to release naturally. Do not depressurize it manually.

16. Open the lid and take the cheesecake out from the instant pot with the help of the trivet handles.

17. Place the pan in the refrigerator for about six hours or overnight. Do not remove the foil and the paper towel from the pan.

18. Once the cake chilled very well, remove the outer spring ring if you are using a spring-form pan and if you are using a push-pan, remove the outer layer of parchment after pushing the bottom up out of the pan.

19. Cut the cake into eight slices.

20. Serve it chilled with whipped cream and cinnamon topping on every slice.

Nutritional values: Calories: 229 | Total Fat: 22g | Saturated Fat: 8g | Total Carbohydrates: 4g | Cholesterol: 64mg | Sodium: 126mg | Potassium: 87mg | Protein: 4g

LOW-CARB CHOCOLATE MINI CAKE

Preparation: 10 minutes | Cooking: 9 minutes | Serves: 2

Ingredients:

- Splenda – 2 tablespoon
- Egg – 2
- Heavy cream – 2 tablespoon
- Baking powder - ½ teaspoon
- Vanilla extract – 1 teaspoon
- Baking cocoa - ¼ cup

Cooking directions:

1. Put all the dry ingredients in a medium bowl and mix.
2. Add egg and mix until it becomes smooth.
3. Spray non-stick cooking oil into the ramekins.
4. Fill each cup half.
5. Cover it with aluminum foil.
6. Pour one cup of water into the Instant Pot.
7. Place a trivet in the cooker and place the cup on the trivet.
8. Close the lid and the vent.
9. Set the Instant Pot to manual high pressure for 9 minutes.
10. When the cooking over, release the pressure manually.
11. Take out the cups and flip onto the plate.
12. Top with Vanilla ice cream and serve.

Nutritional values: Calories: 156 | Fat: 11g | Carbohydrates: 10g | Fiber: 3g | Protein: 7g | Sugars: 3g | Cholesterol: 184mg | Sodium: 71mg | Potassium: 350mg

LOW-CARB VANILLA CHEESECAKE

Preparation: 9 Hours and 10 Minutes | Cooking: 55 Minutes | Serves: 8

Ingredients:

For Filling:

- Cream Cheese kept in room temperature - 16 ounces
- Granulated Swerve - ½ cup + 2 tablespoons
- Vanilla Extract - ½ teaspoon
- Dried Orange Zest, fresh - 1 teaspoon
- Zest of Small Lemon - 1
- Eggs - 3
- Heavy Whipping Cream - ¼ cup

Top Layer:

- Greek Yogurt or Sour Cream full-fat - ½ cup
- Granulated Swerve - 2 teaspoon

Cooking directions

1. Make ready a 6" push pan for preparing the cheesecake.

2. Line a parchment paper all the way around the perimeter of the pan and make sure to place the parchment paper bit taller than the sides of the pan.

3. Now lightly oil the base of the pan.

4. Then, wrap a piece of foil around the bottom of the pan and set aside.

5. The foil covering will help to make sure to check the seepage of cheesecake out of the pan and also it will stop water from entering the cheesecake.

6. In a bowl, using a hand-held mixer, mix the cream, heavy cream cheese, vanilla, Swerve, orange and lemon peels, until it is made soft.

7. Now add eggs into the mixture, one at a time, and gently mix it to get the perfect combination.

8. Do not try to over mix the eggs, or else your cake will be lumpy, instead of creamy.

9. Now pour the filling into the ready pan.

10. Put a paper towel on the pan top and softly wrap up a piece of tin foil over the top to seize the foil in place.

11. Then Pour one or half cups of water into the inner lining pot of your Instant Pot Pressure Cooker and put the stand in the middle of water keeping the handles up.

12. Close the pressure cooker lid and the vent.

13. Push the 'Manual' button to set the time to 37 minutes high pressure cook.

14. While the cake gets ready in the pot, you can prepare the topping.

15. Mix the topping ingredients all together and keep aside.

16. When the whole sequence ends, let the Instant Pot discharge its pressure naturally.

17. When entire pressure released, open the lid.

18. Cautiously lift the cake out of the cooking pot.

19. Take out the paper towel and foil from the top. If any liquid has gathered on top of the cake, gently remove them with a paper towel.

20. While the cake is hot spread the topping over it.

21. Refrigerate the cake for at least eight hours or all night.

22. Cut the cake into 8 slices to serve chilled.

Nutritional values: Calories: 268.1 | Total Fats: 23.8g | Net Carbs: 3g | Protein: 6.8g | Sugars 2.6g | Cholesterol 152.6mg

PRESSURE COOKER KETO CARROT ALMOND CAKE

Preparation time: 10 minutes | Cooking: 50 minutes | Serves: 8

Ingredients:

- Eggs - 3
- Almond flour - 1 cup
- Swerve - ⅔ cup
- Baking powder - 1 teaspoon
- Apple pie spice - 1½ teaspoons
- Coconut oil - ¼ cup
- Heavy whipping cream - ½ cup
- Carrots shredded - 1 cup
- Walnuts chopped - ½ cup

Cooking directions:

1. Take a 6-inch cake pan and grease it.
2. Mix up all ingredients with the help of a hand mixer, until it is well-integrated to look fluffy.
3. Pour the mixture into the oiled pan and cover the pan with an aluminum foil.
4. In the inner liner of the Instant Pot, put two cups of water.
5. Place a steamer rack in the instant pot.
6. Place the foil-covered cake mix on the stand.
7. Now Press the 'cake' button and allow it to cook for at least 40 minutes.
8. Then let the pressure to free naturally for 10 minutes.
9. Let it cool and do the icing of your preference.
10. Serve cool.

Nutritional values: Calories: 268 | Total Fats: 25g | Net Carbs: 6g | Protein: 6g | Sugars: 1g

SHOPPING LIST

Non-Veg items	Beef
	Meat bouillon cubes
	Ground beef
	Venison chuck roast
	Pork
	Boneless chuck roast
	Boneless pork chops
	Pork ribs
	Pork loin chops
	Pork shoulder
	Chicken
	Chicken thighs
	Chicken breast
	Turkish chicken
	Deli Turkey
	Fish
	Prawn
	White fish
	Salmon fillet
	Gurnard fish fillet
	Eggs
	Bacon
	Sausages
	Hot dogs
Vegetables	Onion
	Green cabbage
	Brussel sprouts
	Oyster mushrooms
	Parsley
	Broccoli
	Green chilies
	Baby Bella mushrooms
	Tomatillos
	Jalapeno
	Pecan Halves
	Carrot
	Chives
	Cilantro
	Baby spinach
	Bell pepper
	Yellow onion

		Pitted olives
		Kale heads
		Basil
		Cauliflower
		Zucchini
		Romaine lettuce
		Arugula lettuce
		Chives
		Scallions
		Thyme
		Potato
		Pecans
		Walnuts
		Red bell pepper
		Green bell pepper
		Chipotle pepper
		Celery root
		Leek
	Fruits	Avocado
		Cherry tomatoes
		Dried juniper berries
	Spices	Garlic
		Kielbasa
		Chili powder
		Cumin
		Bay leaf
		Clove
		Oregano
		Black pepper
		Xanthan gum
		Ranch dressing mix
		Italian seasoning mix
		Almond flour
		Onion flakes
		Garlic powder
		Chili powder
		Pepperoncini peppers
		Paprika
		All spice
		Ground coriander
		Ginger
		Turmeric
		Cayenne pepper
		Garam masala
		Jamaican Jerk spice
		Nutmeg

	Cinnamon
	Matcha powder
	Walnuts
	Scallion
	Curry powder
	Dried dill
	Ground mustard
	Dried Rosemary
	Fennel
Liquid and Juice	Lime juice
	Honey
	Water
	Balsamic vinegar
	Beef broth
	Progresso chicken broth
	Chicken broth
	Apple cider vinegar
	Sazon
	Low carb sweetener
	Coconut milk
	Zest of lemon
	Vanilla extract
	Maple syrup (Sugar free)
	Pumpkin puree
	Erythritol
	Almond milk (unsweetened)
	Lakanto Powdered Monk fruit sweetener
	Orange zest
	Pumpkin pie spice
	Splenda
	Greek Yogurt
	Apple pie spice
	White vinegar
	Chicken broth
	White cooking wine
	Vodka
	Collagen protein beef gelatin
Sauce	Adobo
	Marinara sauce
	Tomato paste
	Worcestershire sauce
	Red enchilada sauce
	Tomato paste
	Tamari soy sauce
Salt	Kosher salt
	Sea salt

Cooking oil and other creams	Olive oil
	Coconut oil
	Organic coconut oil
	Butter
	Parmesan cheese
	Ricotta cheese
	Mayonnaise
	Salted butter
	Margarine
	Cream cheese
	Heavy cream
	Half and Half
	Heavy whipping cream
	Sauekraut
	Dulce de Leche
	Truvia
	Ricotta cheese
	Sour cream
	Grass fed butter
	Avocado oil
	Salsa
	Mexican cheese
	Halloumi cheese
	Vegetable oil
	Cheddar cheese
	Smoked cheddar cheese
	Cheese chips
	Crumbled blue cheese
Flour and noodles	Mozzarella
	All-purpose flour
	Coconut flour
	Arrowroot flour
Grains & pulses	Miracle rice
	Sugar
	Cauliflower rice
	Celery seeds
Canned items	Diced tomatoes
	Hearts of Palm
Cookies	Short bread cookies
	Swerve confectioners
	Graham crackers
Baking items	Baking powder
	Baking cocoa
	Tabasco
	Tortillas

KITCHEN APPLIANCES AND UTENSILS USED IN THE RECIPES

Slow Cooker
Instant Pot
Pressure cooker
Food processor
Hand blender
Electric mixer
Knife
Wooden spatula
Non-stick poly-carbon fiber spatula
Stainless steel teaspoons
Stainless steel tablespoons
Wooden spoons
Skillets
Aluminum foils
Kitchen paper towels
Chopping board
Mixing bowls

CONCLUSION

I appreciate and acknowledge every bit of your presence towards this book. I would like to thank you from the bottom of my heart for giving your valuable time to this book and reading it with immense interest.

The ketogenic diet, which is very powerful and helpful in weight loss, is the central theme of this book. Not only does the book highlight the importance of the keto diet, but it also covers the best instant pot ketogenic food recipes that are delicious and mouth-watering. This book is going to make sure that you become younger day by day not only by losing weight but also by enhancing your complexion and health.

An important and interesting fact to note about this book includes the use of instant pot and its applications. Instant pots retain every nutrient of the keto recipes, therefore, making it more healthy and nutritious. Apart from covering a whole lot of information about ketogenic diet this book also contains information on instant pot, which can help a reader to get some basic information about it.

The Do's and Don'ts have mentioned in a separate section of the book. What you can eat and what you should avoid is also covered in this book, which makes it easier for you to follow the diet strictly. Not only does this book help in knowing about ketogenic diet, but it also helps in preparing delicious and healthy food.

Made in the USA
San Bernardino, CA
15 May 2019